Wake Up
Your Bible Study

Also by Richard W. Coffen:
Where Is God When You Hurt?

To order, call 1-800-765-6955.
Visit us at www.reviewandherald.com for information
on other Review and Herald® products.

Wake Up
Your Bible Study

Getting the Most From Your Time With God

{ *Richard W. Coffen* }

Autumn House® Publishing
www.autumnhousepublishing.com
A Division of **REVIEW AND HERALD® PUBLISHING**
Since 1861

Autumn House® titles may be purchased in bulk for educational, business, fund-raising, or sales promotional use. For information, please e-mail SpecialMarkets@reviewandherald.com.

Autumn House® Publishing publishes biblically-based materials for spiritual, physical, and mental growth and Christian discipleship.

The author assumes full responsibility for the accuracy of all facts and quotations as cited in this book.

Texts credited to Anchor are from *Judges (Anchor Bible),* translated and edited by Robert G. Boling. Copyright ©1975 by Doubleday & Co, Inc.

Texts labeled Basic English are from the book *The Bible in Basic English.* Copyrighted in the United States by E. P. Dutton & Co., Inc., 1956.

Scripture quotations marked NASB are from the *New American Standard Bible,* copyright © 1960, 1962, 1963, 1968, 1971, 1972, 1973, 1975, 1977, 1994 by the Lockman Foundation. Used by permission.

Tests credited to NEB are from *The New English Bible.* © The Delegates of the Oxford University Press and the Syndics of the Cambridge University Press 1961, 1970. Reprinted by permission.

Texts credited to NIV are from the *Holy Bible, New International Version.* Copyright © 1973, 1978, 1984, International Bible Society. Used by permission of Zondervan Bible Publishers.

Bible texts credited to NRSV are from the New Revised Standard Version of the Bible, copyright © 1989 by the Division of Christian Education of the National Council of the Churches of Christ in the U.S.A. Used by permission.

Texts credited to Phillips are from J. B. Phillips: *The New Testament in Modern English,* Revised Edition. C J. B. Phillips 1958, 1960, 1972. Used by permission of Macmillan Publishing Co., Inc.

Bible texts credited to RSV are from the Revised Standard Version of the Bible, copyright © 1946, 1952, 1971, by the Division of Christian Education of the National Council of the Churches of Christ in the U.S.A. Used by permission.

Texts credited to Tanakh are from *Tanakh: A New Translation of the Holy Scriptures According to the Traditional Hebrew Texts.* Copyright © The Jewish Publication Society of America, Philadelphia, 1985.

Texts credited to TCNT are from the *Twentieth Century New Testament,* revised edition, Fleming H. Revell Co., 1901.

This book was
Edited by Gerald Wheeler
Copyedited by James Cavil
Cover Design by Trent Truman
Typeset: 11/14 Bembo

PRINTED IN U.S.A.
11   10   09   08   07   5   4   3   2   1

Library of Congress Cataloging-in-Publication Data

Coffen, Richard W.
 Wake Up Your Bible Study : getting the most from your time with God / Richard W. Coffen.
     p. cm.
  ISBN 978-0-8127-0440-2
  1. Bible—Study and teaching. 2. Bible—Hermeneutics. I. Title.
  BS600.3.C64 2007
  220.071—dc22

                              2006102811

Dedicated to

Bob and Ron,
who love God's Word and want to understand it better.

Acknowledgements

The apostle Paul said: "I am a debtor both to Greeks and to barbarians, both to the wise and to the foolish" (Rom. 1:14, NRSV). So am I. It would be impossible to list by name those who have influenced my understanding of God's Word. Every professor I studied under, every Biblicist friend I've chatted with, every scholarly book I've read, every academic lecture I've sat through—all have had an impact on my thinking.

In this book there's not a whole lot that is original with me. I stand upon the shoulders of those who have far more penetrating insights than I do. I've tried to give credit when I've cited another author. However, as we all know, sometimes even our best efforts to give credit where it is due fails. In future editions of this book I shall be pleased to provide sources where I have inadvertently omitted them in this present edition.

Contents

CHAPTER 1

What's a Christian to Do?

W hen my dad became pastor of a new church, one of his early activities was to establish a Berean Club. He'd preach a sermon based on Acts 17:11, which says: "These [the Christians living in Berea] were more noble than those in Thessalonica, in that they received the word with all readiness of mind, and *searched the scriptures daily,* whether those things were so." Dad would challenge the members of his congregation to emulate the Bereans by reading the Bible each day. When they committed to daily Bible study, they thus became inducted into the Berean Club.

Problems in Reading Scripture

If you're like me, ever since childhood you've heard preachers admonish that devout Christians should read the Bible daily. That's good advice, of course. Who would want to argue against such a practice? Would you? Surely I wouldn't! But what about the problems involved in reading Scripture?

What problems? you may ask. How can reading God's Word be problematic? Perhaps we might have problems when it comes to reading other books, but Scripture?

Well, think about it for a moment or two. There actually *are* problems when it comes to reading Sacred Writ.

For example, what version should one use? Some people a generation ago (and the idea is returning with force in some sectors of the church today) insisted that the King James Version (KJV) is the only adequate and appropriate translation.

When I was a young pastoral intern whose assignment was a church near Boston, Massachusetts, I conducted a series of prayer meetings on how to get the most out of studying the Bible. One of the suggestions that I made was to read Scripture from a version other than the KJV. For many of us, we've become so accustomed to the cadence of the Elizabethan English of the KJV that merely reading a different way of saying the same thing can help clarify meaning.

After the meeting ended, elderly Sister Mason cornered me. Wagging a finger knobby with rheumatoid arthritis in my face, she remarked, "You're a good boy and have a good father, but the seminary ruined you!" She proceeded to quote 2 Timothy 3:16 to me: "All scripture is given by inspiration of God."

I had no argument with that passage of Scripture and tried to explain to her in a loud voice—because she was quite hard of hearing—that Paul in this verse was not condemning the use of different versions of the Bible.

But Sister Mason would have none of it! She informed me in no uncertain tones that the KJV is the *one and only* inspired Bible.

At that point a younger member of the congregation sided with Sister Mason, assuring me that "if the King James Version was good enough for Paul, it's good enough for me!" Didn't she know that Paul never saw a KJV—that it did not exist until 1611, long after the Romans beheaded him?

Did you know that nearly two thirds of the wording used in the KJV came largely from Tyndale's translation, which had been published 85 years previously, and from the Bishops' Bible, printed more than 40 years earlier? In other words, the language of the KJV was already somewhat antiquated when the Bible was released. Furthermore, KJV English—Elizabethan English—is not the idiom we use when speaking today. The mere thought of slogging through all those *thees, thous, hasts, dosts, wists,* and other "Quaker" words suffices to scare away all but the most zealous modern reader.

At that time, people considered "thou" and "thee" "familiar" words—that is, words to use when speaking with a single person, especially with a friend. "Thee" and "thou" were not the words one employed when speaking politely to a king or other highborn person. Yet today many Christians assume that it's impolite to use "you" when addressing God in prayer because it seems rude, too chummy. Thus con-

temporary readers might think that they understand what they're reading, but in reality they don't.

Additionally, most people don't realize that a large number of vocabulary words in the KJV today have either dropped from our active word
lists or have evolved different meanings.

Advertise meant "tell" or "inform"; *bark,* to "strip the skin/bark from."
Carriage indicated "baggage." *Daysman* represented a "judge" or "go-
between." *Earing* stood for "plowing"; *fare,* to "rejoice" or "exult." *Gin*
meant a "noose"; *helve,* "handle"; and *implead,* to "accuse." *Jangling* referred to "silly talk." We could proceed through the alphabet, but these
examples should suffice.

Some people argue that there aren't *that* many words that have
changed meaning or dropped from our vocabulary. I suppose they're right.
But the issue is not the number of words that no longer communicate.
Rather the problem is that even a handful of such words can interfere—
even block—communication. When God is trying to reach us, how much
obstruction should we tolerate?

It seems to me that we are blessed today with a plethora of various
translations, each one with its strong and weak points. That's why I like to
compare the wording of any particular Bible verse in numerous versions.
And the footnotes in some of these versions can also provide helpful insights into what the language that the biblical writer used meant.

Reading the Bible is vital. But we're busy people today. How much
time can we squeeze out of our crowded daily schedules to spend with
God's Word? Is five minutes enough? What about 15? Some people argue
that we should set aside at least an hour each day for Bible reading. Part of
the issue, of course, involves priorities. We let a multitude of other activities take precedence over Bible reading.

When I was attending Greater Boston Academy, the topic of daily
Bible reading came up in class. One of the students commented, "When
I begin the day by reading even one verse of Scripture, the rest of the day
goes better." Sally may have been right, but is there really some magical
benefit to reading the Bible?

Admonitions to get up earlier or go to bed later don't cut it for many
of us who already aren't getting enough rest each night, and to continue
that is not healthful. Why add to our intemperance?

Reading or Studying?

Here's something else to consider. Is reading the Bible the same thing as studying it? Wouldn't studying it be preferable to merely reading it? Perhaps at one time or another you decided that you would read the entire Bible through. I made this decision, and tore through the pages of Scripture in a relatively short period of time. Unfortunately, I probably didn't learn much, but at least I met my goal.

Reading the Bible ought to influence the life—if, as we believe, it's God's word to us. But how do we read with understanding? Besides, much of the biblical content is downright boring. We don't find, for instance, the genealogies particularly uplifting. And some of the proverbs seem to contradict each other: "Do not answer a fool according to his folly" (Prov. 26:4, NIV) but "Answer a fool according to his folly" (verse 5, NIV). Which is it?

Maybe if Scripture made more sense to us when we read it, we might find more time to spend with its pages. Usually we can shoehorn into our busy schedules time for something engaging—that which holds meaning for us. Thus we manage to find time to listen to the news on National Public Radio or watch the baseball, basketball, and football games on television. We cram in time to sit and wait in the Olive Garden restaurant while a tasty meal is prepared for us. Even the busiest of us make time to scan *Newsweek* and/or *Time* magazines or the daily newspaper. But much too often we find Bible reading to be insipid. So why bother—especially when what we encounter in its pages often doesn't make a lot of sense?

Furthermore, if we do understand what we're reading in Scripture, some of what we happen upon seems out of touch with the culture in which we live. The words and actions of many biblical characters just don't make much sense to us. And certain parts of Scripture—even the stories, which are theoretically more readable than other portions—just don't resonate for us. Did God really ask Abraham to kill Isaac as a burnt offering (Gen. 22:2)? (Did God demand the violation of the sixth commandment?) Was it really God Himself who commanded that a woman suspected of adultery must drink a distastefully odious potion containing filth scraped from the tabernacle floor in order to discover her guilt or innocence (Num. 5:11-31)? (Isn't that terribly primitive and demeaning for women? Why didn't God require men to do the same?) Did David actually cut off the foreskins of 200 Philistines, presenting them to King Saul as proof of his marriageability (1 Sam. 18:20-27)? (How gory! Aren't you glad you're not a Philistine?) Did God truly send an evil spirit to King Saul (1 Sam. 16:14) and a lying spirit to some prophets (1 Kings 22:22, 23)? (Isn't it the *Holy* Spirit who comes from God, not an evil or lying one?) Why did Daniel pray in front of his open windows, where he knew he'd be seen . . . and prosecuted (Dan. 6:10)? (Didn't Jesus tell us to go into the closet to pray [Matt. 6:6]?) Did God really truly slay Ananias and Sapphira when they didn't give to the church all the money they had pledged (Acts 5:1-10)? (How vengeful of Him!)

We're Not All Scholars

How can we Christians in the pew *study* Scripture? That's something scholars do. Right? Studying implies research. Most of us aren't trained in the techniques of biblical research. Few of us can read the three languages the Bible was originally written in—Hebrew, Aramaic, and Greek. Almost none of us have mastered the grammar and syntax of those ancient languages. Nor are we historians who know the details of what went on in the ancient Near Eastern world. And we haven't received training in exegesis (extracting meaning from texts) and hermeneutics (applying meaning from texts—as in sermons).

That kind of thing is for the academicians—at least a certain group of scholars. (Scholars with degrees in other disciplines—American history, botany, astronomy, nuclear physics, mathematics, psychology, medicine, English literature—can find reading the Scriptures just as daunting as any other person in the pew.)

All of us want to take God's Word seriously, but whether we read it or even study it, for that matter, we want to be sure that we understand it correctly. Even if we don't have formal training in biblical interpretation. What use is studying Scripture if we come up with fanciful, harebrained understandings of what it says? We've all met sincere people who've developed off-the-wall explanations of biblical passages. Even educated people can come up with just as many bizarre explanations of what they read in Scripture as someone with only a third-grade education.

So maybe we ordinary Christians need to find a compromise between a superficial reading of the Bible and in-depth study of it. While we don't want to read it like a child, yet at the same time we can't possibly delve into its depths like a professor. There must be a middle ground somewhere. Maybe this book can aid you in your study of God's Word.

Through the years I've learned—largely as a result of my dabbling in scholarly pursuits—a few ways of making some sense out of what I read in Scripture. Space does not permit us to look at every aspect of Bible study, but we will explore a few of them, including some aspects that you may never have encountered before. Perhaps some of them will help you find more meaning in your reading of God's Word than you've previously experienced.

CHAPTER 2

What Does It Say and What Does It Mean?

D on't interpret for me anything that you read in the Bible. Just tell
me what it says. OK?" Victor instructed.

Have you ever heard someone say something like this—even though
the words may not have been identical, but the gist was similar? You've
probably seen the bumper sticker that reads: "The Bible says it, and I believe it." But even though a certain amount of truth underlies it, such a
position has a fundamental problem. In this chapter we'll explore briefly
both the problem and the truth inherent in the admonition.

The Inherent Problem

The problem with wanting simply to read the Bible but not to interpret it is that *the very process of reading is an act of interpretation.* That is a
fact inherent in the nature of language itself. Language is not directly
connected to what it seeks to communicate. Let me explain. Verbal
sounds, for instance, are generally unrelated to what they signify. The
clear liquid that pours from a faucet is pronounced *water* in English, *eau*
in French, *agua* in Spanish, *vatten* in Swedish, *apa* in Romanian, *nusc* in
Vietnamese, *mul* in Korean, *omi* in Yoruba, *amanzi* in Zulu, and *mayim*
in biblical Hebrew. Clearly these words have no necessary connection
with the liquid chemical H_2O. Furthermore, the squiggles that we call
letters of the alphabet and their combination used to represent H_2O (or
any other word, for that matter) are arbitrary.

Vocal sounds (phonemes) and their written form (alphabetical letters)

17

as they are combined into words are nearly always arbitrary. A few words do appear to have some logical connection with their referents, and we refer to these as onomatopoetic terms: *gurgle, babble, oink, meow, baa,* and *bow wow,* for example. But even onomatopoetic words for the same sound are not always identical from one language to another, making it nearly impossible for someone to anticipate what specific onomatopoetic sound a given language will use. You may even find it difficult to link an onomatopoetic sound to its referent after hearing it.

The following examples of various animal sounds as rendered in several different languages show that while onomatopoetic agreement may exist in some languages, widespread differences can exist in what we would assume should be similar renderings for identical sounds.

Here's what a dog says: *bow wow* (English), *ham ham* (Albanian), *haw haw* (Arabic), *wang wang* (Mandarin Chinese), *hau hau* (Finnish), *ouah ouah* (French), *gonggong* (Indonesian), *wanwan* (Japanese), and *gav-gav* (Russian). Notice that the one constant here is a double syllable, yet even that is not consistent throughout all languages, including English (*woof* and *arf*).

Here's what a hen says: *cluck cluck* (English), *ka ko ko ko* (Albanian), *cout cout cout* (Arabic), *gok-gok* (Danish), *cotcotcodet* (French), *ka-ka-ka* (Greek), *kokekokkoo* (Japanese), *kko-kko-daek-kko-kko-kko-kko* (Korean), and *cuc-cuc tac* (Vietnamese).

From these simple examples (I won't bore you with more), we can understand the logic behind such onomatopoetic words, but the variety of these sounds is somewhat surprising. We can detect some imitation of sounds, even though the choice of these imitative words is somewhat arbitrary, making it quite hard to anticipate in advance what the sound will be.

Apart from just the individual vocabulary words, the gathering of words into sentences can also be somewhat arbitrary. In the English language we typically expect a certain word order in a sentence: adjective, noun (subject) and adverb, verb (predicate). For example: **The angry** (adjective) **dog** (noun) **viciously** (adverb) **barked** (verb). Good English would not allow us to write: **The barked viciously dog angry** or **The barked dog angry viciously.**

But such a strict ordering of words isn't necessarily the word order commonly employed in other languages. In Greek, for instance, the verb can come first (thereby emphasizing the action), followed by the noun subject, then, in turn, an adverb (modifying the verb) and an adjective (modifying the noun).

This scrambled (to our modern Western way of thinking) word order isn't all that confusing because the various Greek words are "inflected," which means that a given word will have a special ending that depends on its role in a sentence. If a noun is the subject of the sentence, it will have a different ending than if it functions as the direct object of the verb. An adjective modifying a noun will have an ending that corresponds to the ending of the noun it describes. Likewise, an adverb will "agree" with the verb it modifies. Thus word order isn't all that crucial for the syntax of a sentence in biblical Greek (known among scholars as koine Greek).

Whether one is reading something written in English or Greek or Hebrew doesn't matter; the reader must constantly interpret during the act of reading. One simply cannot read without interpreting. The rules of grammar and syntax require interpretation on the part of readers.

Sentences grammatically and syntactically correct also require interpretation. What does this sentence mean? "Oh, I just *love* ice cream!" Do you infer from this cluster of six words that the speaker likes or dislikes ice cream? The sentence in itself can mean either. Readers must decide whether the speaker is stating a fact or is being facetious.

Often the larger context helps a reader sense the meaning of an ambiguous sentence. Was the statement "Oh, I just *love* ice cream!" spoken in the context of an invitation to eat at the local ice-cream parlor? Did that invitation come from a friend? Was it made by someone who knew the other's preferences and for spite suggested a visit to the local Dairy Queen? Sometimes the context itself is so ambiguous that a reader cannot come to any clear and certain conclusion. When that happens, the reader must leave open all possible interpretations.

Whether we are listening to others speak or reading words printed on paper, for any communication to occur we must interpret the symbols that we hear or see. That's how we make sense of what others say. In fact, that's what communicating is all about—extracting sense from the symbols others utter or write. And that process of digging out meaning from these signs (I'm using the words "signs" and "symbols" interchangeably) we call interpretation.

The Inherent Truth

There is, however, truth inherent in Victor's request: "Don't interpret for me anything that you read in the Bible. Just tell me what it says."

We can easily forget that there's a difference between what a Bible writer asserted and what that assertion means. In fact, Krister Stendahl, well-known Lutheran biblical scholar and specialist in Paul's writings, famously indicated that we should differentiate what a biblical passage says, what it meant (back then—for the original recipients), and what it means (today—for us). It is a helpful distinction to keep in mind as we study the Bible.

Textual Criticism—The study of what a biblical writer said in any given passage includes what academicians call "textual criticism," also once known as "lower criticism." In fact, when I studied theology in college and at the seminary, my conservative professors insisted that lower criticism was a legitimate field of study for those who love Scripture, whereas higher criticism was a dangerous area of study for evangelical Christians. (The word "criticism" in this context does not refer to a negative practice of tearing down but is an academic term to describe scholarly evaluation of data in a discipline or area of study.)

Textual critics look at the various manuscripts that have come down to us and try to determine (through a set of rigorous criteria) what the original autograph would have contained. ("Autograph" is the word that biblical scholars use for the original documents written by Moses, Jeremiah, Luke, Paul, etc.) Because no biblical autographs still exist, the only documents that textual critics have to work with are copies of copies of copies—all painstakingly handwritten.

According to Bart D. Ehrman, University of North Carolina's chair of the Department of Religious Studies, within the corpus of both Old and New Testament manuscripts "the 5,700 manuscripts of the Greek New Testament that have been catalogued contain more variations than there are words in the New Testament" (in *Bible Review*, Winter 2005, p. 17). Depending on how a scholar determines what is a variant (Do two differences in one word count as one or two variances?), he sees "200,000 variant readings" while others contend that there are 300,000 or even 400,000 variants (*ibid.*).

But before you become too alarmed over this huge number, you need to know that most of the differences have little or no real impact on the meaning of the text. Often they consist of different spellings (standardization of spelling is something relatively new in human history), substitution of a synonym (a word that means the same thing), use of a homonym (words that sound the same but have a different meaning; they crept in because many scribes copied manuscripts by listening to someone dictate them), additions to the text, deletions to the text, grammatical changes, and variations in word order, among other things. Ehrman reminds us "that scribes could not always spell or keep focused" (*ibid.*).

For instance, sometimes a scribe or even a reader might add a comment of agreement in the margin of a document. Since this was the same method for correcting an inadvertent omission, the next copyist just might incorporate the marginal comment as part of the text, not realizing that it was just a comment. Such additions are easy to spot when the handwriting of the original marginal comment is different from that of the scribe who prepared the entire manuscript. Other times, detecting such insertions is more difficult.

A New Testament example of a marginal comment that became embedded in the text itself appears in Matthew's version of the Lord's Prayer, which ends "for thine is the kingdom, and the power, and the glory, for ever" (Matt. 6:13). The words do not occur in Luke's rendition of the same prayer (Luke 11:2-4), and the scholarly consensus is that they were a scribal comment that came to be inserted into the original text. The earliest (oldest) manuscripts do not contain them. So when we find these words omitted in other versions of Scripture, it isn't a result of some atheistic plot to undermine faith in God. Bible translators do not include the above words because scholars agree that Jesus most likely did not say them when He taught His disciples to pray.

Ehrman points out one New Testament verse with a variant that can be quite significant. Mark 1:41 tells us that "Jesus, moved with compassion, put forth his hand, and touched him, and saith unto him, I will; be thou clean." The words in question are "moved with compassion." The majority of copies of the Gospel of Mark use a word that we can properly translate as "having compassion." However, a few ancient manuscripts use a different word—one that means that Jesus got angry rather than was moved with pity.

Most scholars opt for the wording in the majority of documents, but

Ehrman belongs to the minority. He explains the positions of both the majority and the minority of textual critics, but he feels that originally the text said that Jesus became irate. A later scribe changed the text so that Christ wouldn't be angry, which to him probably seemed rather heretical. Because in other passages and Gospels Jesus was said to have had compassion, this unknown (and hypothetical) scribe changed Mark 1:41 so that it would indicate Jesus' compassion rather than anger.

Whether Jesus became angry or sympathetic, one has to account for the discrepancy somehow, and it makes sense that at one point a scribe either changed the description of Jesus' feelings from compassion to anger or from anger to compassion.

Especially when it comes to numbers, we frequently find discrepancies in parallel passages or in ancient versions. Those who try to prepare chronologies from the information given in the biblical text face a monumental task. For example, when one adds up the various ages of the patriarchs given in Genesis 5, the resulting elapsed time spans differ depending on whether one uses the ages given in the Masoretic text (the traditional Hebrew Bible), the Septuagint (the official Greek translation of the Hebrew Scriptures made by ancient Hebrew scholars, which was the biblical text cited most often by the New Testament writers), or the Samaritan Pentateuch (another old text but cherished by the Samaritans, a rival religion of Judaism, which still has a few adherents). Which of them should a student of chronology use?

On several occasions, Jewish copyists purposely substituted one Hebrew word for another in order to protect God's reputation, so to speak. The rabbinical Hebrew term for such emendations is *tikkun sofrim*, which means "fixed by the sages" or scribes. The original wording seemed just too sacrilegious. The rabbis tell us of at least 11 instances of this—and they identify them. However, we have reason to suspect that there may be at least a few other instances of the same thing.

Here's an example of such a change. The biblical passage says that "Abraham stood yet before the Lord" (Gen. 18:22). However, the rabbis tell us that the original text said that "the Lord [YHWH] stood before Abraham." The scribes considered it preposterous that God would stand before Abraham, because that indicates that YHWH was somehow subordinate to Abraham. So the sages "fixed" the text, making it read as it does today in the KJV so that it is Abraham who is inferior to God.

Here's another example. Zechariah 2:8 states: "He that toucheth you toucheth the apple of his eye." According to rabbinic tradition, the text originally read: "toucheth the apple of God's eye." But again, out of respect for God, the scribes changed the possessive from "God's" to "his." Notice, though, that it really doesn't change the intent of the passage.

In the following example, the scribes have altered the meaning of the text. Job 32:3 tells us that "against his three friends was his [Job's] wrath kindled, because they had found no answer, and yet had condemned Job." That's how the sages made the text read when they copied it. However, the original had said that "they had found no answer, and yet had condemned God." The scribes considered condemning God to be blasphemous, so they "fixed" the text and had Job's friends condemning him instead.

There is more to arriving at the original wording than merely comparing and analyzing ancient handwritten documents. Biblical scholars also bring to the text their expertise in understanding the Hebrew, Aramaic, and Greek languages. For example, did the original author actually use poor grammar in certain passages, or did the text become corrupted through repeated copying?

Exegesis—The skill (some might say "science") of determining what a passage meant to its original recipients is called "exegesis." Exegetes, as we sometimes refer to these interpreters, have trained in a cluster of abilities that includes facility in reading Hebrew, Aramaic, and Greek; experience in deciding which manuscript probably resembles most closely the original autograph; familiarity with the "semantic range" or spectrum of possible meanings of a given Hebrew, Aramaic, or Greek word; acquaintance with the customs of the ancient Near Eastern culture; recognition of how human beings use language; an understanding of various literary genres (types of writing—laws, songs, diatribes, lawsuits, epistles, gospels, etc.); and other learned skills.

Hermeneutics—The art of applying to one's present-day situation what was originally said thousands of years ago is called "hermeneutics." Many pastors took a class in college or seminary that taught the art of interpreting a biblical passage in light of contemporary culture.

The end result of applied hermeneutics is the sermon. Persons trained in hermeneutics use some of the same skills involved in exegesis. But they take their work one step further. In addition to determining what the scriptural text *meant* (past tense—what a reader contemporary with Isaiah or with Paul understood the text to say), they also try to figure out what it *means* (present tense—what modern readers can "take away" from the text). What the text meant and what it means may not always be identical, but the latter should not contradict the former.

What the Bible Writers Said,
What They Meant, and What It Means

Perhaps a few examples might help us understand the distinction between what the Bible writers said and what the text meant. (Because this book is not a sermon, we won't be especially concerned with what a passage or biblical document means to us today.)

What the Bible says—literally says—is not the same as our *interpretation* of what it declares. This may seem like a very simple distinction (and it is), but it is something that many people either do not recognize or do not understand.

Here are some concrete examples for you to consider.

Exodus 20:10—The Bible says, quite literally: "The seventh day is the sabbath"—Saturday.

Once various denominations argued over which day of the week is the Sabbath. Nowadays it's hardly a matter of debate. Even Pope John Paul II himself in his apostolic letter titled *Dies Domini* freely admitted that the biblical Sabbath is the seventh day of the week—the day just before Sunday. He talked about the origin of the Sabbath at the end of Creation week, when God rested from His creative work and blessed the seventh day (Chapter I, sections 8-17). Then he referred to "the first day after the Sabbath" and talked about moving "from the 'Sabbath' to the 'first day after the Sabbath,' from the seventh day to the first day" (I, 18; II, 21).

Few debate anymore over which day is the biblical Sabbath. Contemporary biblical and systematic theologians are clear—the seventh day (Saturday) is the biblical Sabbath.

The argument is over. We all agree on what the Bible says.

But what does this mean? Nowadays the discussion is about what significance the biblical Sabbath has for contemporary Christians. Many theologians tend to treat the Sabbath in the same manner as they do circumcision—something that the Jews did, but that is not necessary for Christians to observe.

John 14:2—According to Jesus' own words, what is He "building" in heaven for us?

He's building what? Houses? Mansions? Read the verse: "In my Father's house are many mansions."

Notice that Jesus mentions two things: "house" (singular) and "mansions" (plural). Note also the tense of the verb Jesus uses: "In my Father's house *are* [present tense] many mansions."

Think about what Jesus was saying here. The word translated "mansions" does not refer to palatial domiciles but to merely a place to stay. The Romans used "mansion" to refer to what we would call hotels or travel lodges. It could refer to a room within a larger structure. Maybe just a corner of a room, with a mat for a bed. Even the stable where Jesus was born could be such a place—a place to stay.

And Jesus doesn't say that He would build big houses for us. Rather, He says that He would *prepare* a place to stay—that is, He would *make ready* a place to stay. Perhaps we could say that He would tidy up a place for us—whether that be a house, a room, or a corner.

That's what this famous verse of Scripture *says*. So now that we are clear on what it says, what does the passage *mean*?

Jesus is speaking in the context of His Father's house, so He's talking about family. Because we're members of His family, He was leaving to make ready a place for us to stay so that He could come back and take us home with Him. It is the Father—His Father and our Father—who has the large house. But as members of the family, we're always welcome because Jesus has tidied up a place for us. And when it comes to family, there's always room for one more—Jesus can always find another cubbyhole for us to call our own, where we can stay.

1 Corinthians 15:29—The passage literally *says:* "Else what shall they do which are baptized for the dead, if the dead rise not at all? why are they then baptized for the dead?"

Just in case you're wondering, the KJV is an almost word-for-word translation. In other words, this particular English wording is an accurate rendition of what the Greek text *says*.

There's just one exception, and it is really not significant. The KJV rendering mentions "baptized for the dead" two times. Although Paul refers to being baptized for the dead twice in this verse, the second time he does not use the expression "the dead" but rather the pronoun "them"—being baptized for "them." But since the antecedent is clearly "the dead," the King James translators took the liberty of replacing the word "them" with "the dead." It merely adds clarity to the rendition.

So far we have established what the text *says*. Now let's talk about its interpretation.

First Corinthians 15 deals with the validity of resurrection. Paul begins the discussion here by talking about the resurrection of Jesus. Next, the apostle names the witnesses of the resurrected Jesus. Cephas—Peter—saw Him. Then the twelve. Later about 500 people witnessed that He was alive. Then James and, following that, all the apostles observed Him. Last of all, Paul claims to have seen the resurrected Jesus.

The resurrected Jesus was a public figure. Despite this evidence, Paul points out that some of the Corinthian Christians were insisting that no resurrection ever happened or was possible. So Paul begins heaping more logical evidence upon logical evidence to further build his case that there is indeed such a thing as resurrection.

1. If the Corinthians are correct that there is no resurrection, then Christ did not rise from the dead.
2. If Christ was not raised, then the apostles' preaching was in vain.
3. If their preaching was in vain, then the believers' faith would also be in vain.
4. But if their faith was in vain, then they'd still be lost in sin.
5. And those duped Christians who had already died had perished—hopelessly perished forever.
6. And if our hope is only in this life and this world, then we are surely miserable—to be pitied for our misplaced trust.

Paul next proclaims the wonders of resurrection. The glorified Jesus will be conqueror of all—even of death, the last enemy He will subdue.

The apostle then adds another argument to support belief in resurrection. Some of the Corinthian Christians were being baptized for the dead. But why would they do such a thing if there were no resurrection? What they were doing assumes its reality. Such a practice would have no meaning otherwise.

After that argument from one of their customs, Paul produces still another line of reasoning. Why would the apostles constantly risk life and limb to spread the word about a resurrection if such a thing was not real? It would be stupid of them to place their lives in jeopardy in the face of total and utter dissolution—with no hope of resurrection should they be killed.

Paul then proceeds to explain what kind of body a resurrected body is. It will not be identical with our present physical, material bodies. While it will still be a body, it will be a spiritual body, a glorified body, a much superior one. He uses an analogy: there is continuity between a seed and the mature plant that sprouts from it, but there is also discontinuity. The acorn is not identical with the oak tree. So the body that we bury is sown in a corruptible form, but God will raise it in an incorruptible form. Though it is sown as a natural body, God transforms it into a spiritual one (spiritual does not mean immaterial or invisible).

The apostle concludes by almost singing about the resurrection to come. What will happen is a mystery. We will not all sleep, but we will all be changed, glorified. And this will take place at the trumpet call announcing the Second Coming. Through Jesus death itself will be swallowed up in victory.

So in this verse Paul uses what the Corinthian Christians themselves were doing—being baptized for the dead—as an argument to defeat their reasoning that there is no such thing as resurrection. Their behavior and their theology contradicted each other.

But what was this quaint practice of being baptized for the dead? We simply do not know. Students of the Bible have come up with more than 200 explanations or interpretations.

Most, but not all, agree that Paul was referring to some kind of vicarious baptism. But what? And why?

Imagine—more than 200 attempts to explain its meaning! No wonder F. W. Grosheide says that this verse "is one of the most difficult passages in the New Testament" (*Commentary on the First Epistle to the Corinthians*, p. 371).

Not only do scholars not know what it *meant*, but also most are puzzled about what it *means*. Except the Mormons. They actually baptize members in behalf of or for the benefit of their deceased relatives.

First Corinthians 15:29 is a real poser for most Christians. We know what the Bible *says*. But we don't know what it *meant*. And we sure haven't a clue as to what it *means* for us today.

I hope that by now you can see the distinction between what the Bible *says* and what it means or what we say it means. The literal wording of Scripture is not always easily aligned with our interpretation of it. And the problem is that the act of interpretation is not an option that we can take or leave as we wish. Every biblical passage must be interpreted—just as we must interpret everything we read . . . and hear . . . and see.

It is naive to think that meaning is totally inbuilt in the very words themselves. Clusters of words—sentences and paragraphs, we call them—must be interpreted. So let me repeat myself, even at the risk of becoming redundant: what the Bible *says* is one thing and what it *means* is another matter. The two are not the same. They may be related—and must be—but they are not one and the same thing.

So when people come up with interpretations of scriptural passages that differ from our traditional understandings, that does not *necessarily* mean that they do not believe in the authority of the Bible. Nor does it *necessarily* indicate that they are in rebellion against God's Word, are under the influence of satanic doubt, or are spurning God and His wisdom. They are not *necessarily* evil persons out to destroy God's kingdom.

Rather, it just might mean that they are taking God's Word very seriously, but their conclusions about its meaning do not coincide with ours. While they might not be what we would call "traditional," that doesn't necessarily mean they are sinister. So it would behoove us to refrain from name-calling, casting aspersions on their integrity, and second-guessing their motives.

What the Bible says and what we say it means are thus two separate matters, even though they have a close connection. That's something I think every Bible reader must always keep in mind.

CHAPTER 3

The Truth About Sound Bites

Y ou've undoubtedly heard this expression. It's such a relatively new term that authorities have not yet agreed on how it should be spelled. Most of us at this point in time would probably use two words—sound bite. But according to Wikipedia, which identifies itself as "the free encyclopedia" on the Internet, it should be spelled as one word—soundbite.

Just exactly what is a sound bite? I keyed the word into Google, and several definitions appeared on the screen, all of which agreed with one another even though the wording differed.

Videomaker magazine said that it is "any short recorded audio segment for use in an edited program—usually a highlight taken from an interview."

CNN defined it this way: "In the reporting of TV news, a very short statement, lasting no more than a few seconds, that tries to convey a specific idea, image, or perception that will attract the viewing audience's attention."

I found a relatively long section on sound bites (at least when compared with the very terse defintions my Google search came up with) in Wikipedia. (*Wiki wiki* is Hawaiian for "quick." Ward Cunningham says, "I chose wiki-wiki as an alliterative substitute for 'quick' and thereby avoided naming this stuff 'quick-web'." A wiki is thus a Web site that is a source of quick information. Additionally, it's a site that people can edit.) The information given included this sentence: "In film and broadcasting, a soundbite is a very short piece of footage taken from a longer speech or an interview in which someone with authority . . . says something which is considered by those who edit the speech or interview to be the most important point."

Wikipedia even gave some examples to illustrate exactly what a sound bite is. President Ronald Reagan uttered a well-remembered sound bite: "Mr. Gorbachev, tear down this wall!" He was, of course, referring to the infamous Berlin Wall, which ultimately did get demolished.

Another example cited: "Houston, Tranquility Base here. The *Eagle* has landed." The Apollo 11 moon landing had become a reality, and this is what Neil Armstrong said when the lunar module touched down on the lunar surface at 4:18 p.m. EDT on July 20, 1969. And at 10:56 p.m. EDT that same day, as he set foot on the surface of the moon itself—the first human being ever to walk on the moon—he said, "That's one small step for a man, one giant leap for mankind."

Sound Bites From the Bible

Theoretically, a sound bite is supposed to express the very essence of the larger story in which the notable and quotable words are embedded. "Such key moments in dialogue (or monologue) stand out better in the audience's memory and thus become the 'taste' that best represents the entire 'meal' of the larger message or conversation" (Wikipedia).

Let me share with you a few examples of what I consider to be prime examples of *accurate* sound bites from Scripture. See if you agree with me that these instances are faithful to the overall message of the Bible.

"For God so loved the world, that he gave his only begotten Son, that whosoever believeth in him should not perish, but have everlasting life" (John 3:16). It is perhaps the most well-known Bible verse—at least among Christians. I think it's fair to say that the passage encapsulates well the message of the Gospel of John. In fact, one can argue cogently that as a sound bite John 3:16 is faithful to the message of the entire New Testament— perhaps even the entire body of Scripture.

Here's an example from the Old Testament. "What doth the Lord require of thee, but to do justly, and to love mercy, and to walk humbly with thy God?" (Micah 6:8). The passage fairly sums up the social consciousness that lies behind the messages of the Hebrew prophets. Sir George Adam Smith, a Scottish Old Testament scholar who taught at the United Free Church College in Glasgow, Scotland, from 1892 to 1909, wrote: "This is the greatest saying of the Old Testament" (cited by Francis I. Andersen and David Noel Freedman in *The Anchor Bible on Micah*, vol. 24E, p. 504).

As a sound bite, "Faith is the substance of things hoped for, the evidence of things not seen" (Heb. 11:1) fairly sums up the content of the great faith chapter. Hebrews 11 says a lot more, of course, but the verse is an excellent précis of the entire chapter.

Here's a little exercise that you may enjoy doing. Take your Bible and open it at random. Read carefully the chapter you turned to, and then select the verse within that chapter or story or thought that you feel is a good sound bite—one that is true to the content of that particular chapter, story, or unit. (It may be that some units just don't have a sound bite available. If so, try again in another portion of Scripture.) In fact, why not try this exercise with some friends? Have everyone look at the same scriptural passage, and see if all of you agree on which verse or fragment is the best sound bite for the selected section.

I just tried this experiment, and ended up at Psalm 111. This song of only 10 verses has several main emphases packed into it. I finally decided that the fourth verse contained a sound bite worthy of the entire psalm. Either the first or the last half of that verse seemed to work well. Finally I decided on the following as an appropriate sound bite: "The Lord is gracious and full of compassion."

The Proof-Text Approach

It would be helpful if all sound bites—secular or otherwise—were wise summations of what is being said in the larger context. However, many times a sound bite might be truly catchy but not really express the core meaning of the entire newsworthy item. And that's the danger of sound bites. They can readily distort rather than express truth. The Wikipedia article on sound bites points this out. "As the context of what is being said is missing, the insertion of soundbites into news broadcasts or documentaries is open to manipulation and thus requires a very high degree of journalistic ethics." And if the person selecting the sound bite lacks a "very high degree of journalistic ethics," the sound bite could mislead those who hear it.

Speakers who have suffered sound bite victimization often will protest: "Yes, I said those words, but they have been taken out of context. What I meant is . . ." It can be extremely frustrating to fall victim to sound biting. Perhaps you yourself have had someone quote you out of context. It's even possible that the sound bite leaves others with the impression that you said just the opposite of what you really meant.

Sound bites extracted from their larger contexts by someone without a "very high degree of journalistic ethics" can have dire consequences. If, for example, you want to know what someone running for public office stands for, you must be sure that your judgment of him or her does not rest on sound bites that the news media may have taken out of their original context. Take the time and invest the effort into studying the entire speech so that you'll be able to judge fairly what the speaker truly meant by what he or she said.

When it comes to selecting sound bites from Scripture, we want to be especially careful, for none of us wants to be guilty of distorting the Word of God. The fact is, however, that many of us (and I include myself) have done this. Often we treat the Bible as though it were a collection of aphorisms—divinely inspired pithy sayings. We therefore wrench verses from their original setting, making them say that which the Bible writer never intended. Such an approach to Scripture is often called proof-texting, and seminary teachers warn their students against the unfortunate practice. Proof-texting is especially common in Bible studies and evangelistic sermons, and is usually employed in order to make a doctrinal point. Sadly, if the speaker is not scrupulously careful, he or she might make biblical passages say that which the inspired Bible writer never had in mind.

Perhaps a few common examples will demonstrate what I'm talking about.

Before Terri Schiavo died on March 31, 2005, many protestors gathered outside the hospice where she was staying and demanded that she remain on life support. Crowds of well-meaning people waved signs and shouted warnings that condemned any activity that might end up leading to her death. Terri Schiavo was at the center of a firestorm fueled by religion and politics—a volatile mix.

Once the courts ruled that her life-support system could be shut off, the rhetoric became even more strident. You may recall that even the U.S. Congress tried to get into the act. Outside the hospice where Ms. Schiavo lay in her unconscious state and after life-support measures had been terminated, one protestor held a sign that said, "I thirst." These were among Jesus' last words as He hung on the cross, as you know.

But what did those words of the dying Jesus have to do with Terri Schiavo? They weren't a biblical promise that some well-meaning person might claim in prayer. Nor did they constitute a prophecy of some future event, namely Ms. Schiavo's imminent death from starvation and dehydration. Rather they were simply an expression of our Lord's physical need while He hung on the cross, the sacrificial Lamb of God who takes away the sins of the world. Jesus, not Terri Schiavo, is our Savior. What He uttered on the cross on that Good Friday nearly 2,000 years ago had no direct connection with the ethical drama played out in Florida.

Waving a placard that said "I thirst" outside Schiavo's hospice was an illegitimate employment of a sound bite from Scripture—in short, this sort of proof-texting is worse than just not being helpful. It's downright dishonest. The quotation might fan the flames of passion over the case of a dying Floridian, but it is surely an inept use of the Bible. In this particular modern situation those two words from the Gospel of John (19:28) were meaningless.

Here's another example to think about.

In 1968 Dr. C. Everett Koop lost his son, David, a student at Dartmouth College, who fell to his death while climbing a mountain. His body lay outside, exposed to the elements, for 52 hours before rescuers could reach him. Dr. Koop, who maintains a strongly held belief in predestination, wrote a book about his jarring loss. He closed the book, titled *Sometimes Mountains Move,* by citing Jude 24: "Now unto him that is able to keep you from falling . . ." and ended with the words: "God was able, but in His sovereignty He chose not to" (cited by Philip Yancey, *Soul Survivor*, p. 182).

Is this what Jude was talking about—that God could have kept David Koop from falling off the cliff (but somehow in His inscrutable purposes failed to do so)? No, of course not! Jude 24 is talking about falling into sin—not falling from precipices. This sound bite—or proof-texting—used by Dr. Koop might sound pious, but it misconstrues Jude's inspired intent. Perhaps we can excuse Dr. Koop because his expertise lies in an area other than biblical interpretation. However, despite my respect for this former surgeon general and since he is extremely proficient in the English language, he should have read the context of Jude 24 and ended his book short of citing this sound bite from the Bible.

Poor Richard's Almanack, a book from which we can isolate independent wise sayings, is full of sound bites, although Benjamin Franklin surely would not have understood that terminology. Here are a few of the pithy apothegms, as Franklin called them, from that classic book. "Beware of the young doctor and the old barber." "Hunger never saw bad bread." "Visits should be short, like a winter's day; lest you're too troublesome, hasten away."

However, the Bible is not an inspired version of Franklin's *Poor Richard's Almanack*, a book into which we can randomly dip and extract clever sound bites that titillate the mind. The only portion of Scripture that we could use that way is the book of Proverbs, which usually gives us wise sayings that are generally just a verse or two long. They *do* make good sound bites, and we're probably not misusing Scripture when we skip around in the book of Proverbs, blithely ignorant of any context.

Some, though, argue that the proof-text method is indeed *the* approach to Bible study—especially giving Bible studies to people interested in what a particular church believes. In fact, that's the format of most Bible studies and Bible lesson courses: (1) pose a question and (2) reply with a Bible verse. A chain of this sequence is what we normally call a "Bible study," and some insist that it is the best way to convince others of specific doctrines. But consider the following Bible study. Do you agree with all the conclusions formed by the proof-text method?

1. **How many gods are there?** 1 Corinthians 8:5—Many.
2. **Are all these gods equally worthy of worship?** Exodus 20:3—No, they must not take precedence over YHWH, the true God.
3. **Why is YHWH more worthy than other gods?** 2 Chronicles 2:5—He is greater than they.
4. **How are these other gods to relate to Him?** Psalm 97:7—They are to worship Him.
5. **What is the difference between these gods and YHWH?** Psalm 96:5—They are idols; He created the heavens.
6. **Who, then, can rightfully be called the Creator?** Isaiah 40:28—The everlasting God, YHWH.
7. **What will happen to the non-Creator gods?** Jeremiah 10:11—They will perish.
8. **How much did YHWH make?** Isaiah 44:24—All things—not

some things, not most things, but *all* things.

9. **Did YHWH make the stars?** Job 9:9—Yes.

10. **Did He make the sun and moon?** Genesis 1:16—Yes.

11. **Did He make the heaven and the earth and the sea also?** Psalm 146:6—Yes.

12. **What did God do about the sea?** Job 38:8-11—He set its bounds beyond which it cannot go; thus He is responsible for where the ocean waves go, because they can do nothing without His guidance.

13. **Did YHWH create the earth in vain?** Isaiah 45:18—No.

14. **Did He create human being as well as beast?** Jeremiah 27:5—Yes.

15. **Did God create human beings in vain?** Psalm 89:47—Yes.

16. **Did He create the rain?** Job 28:26—Yes. So He is responsible for the amount of rain we get, since He sends it. (Obviously, then, He is responsible for floods and for drought.)

17. **Did YHWH create the lightning and wind?** Jeremiah 10:13—Yes. He is responsible for them. (Then He must be responsible for what the lightning and wind do—storm damage.)

18. **Did God make the seasons?** Psalm 74:17—Yes. He created the summer and winter.

19. **Did He make anything else?** Proverbs 16:4—Yes. God made all things—including the wicked.

20. **God made the wicked? Doesn't God create only good things? Did He really make evil?** Isaiah 45:7—Yes, God makes evil.

21. **What about the blind and mute? Who creates these people with birth defects?** Exodus 4:11—God does.

22. **Who creates the cripples?** Numbers 5:21—God does.

23. **Is it fair to expect only good from God?** Job 2:10—No. Job says that it isn't logical to expect good but not bad from Him.

24. **What else did God make?** Exodus 15:25—He made statutes and laws.

25. **What kind of laws did God make?** Ezekiel 20:25—God made laws that were not good. Some were even against us—Colossians 2:14.

What do you think about that Bible study? It seems to have started out OK. In fact, you probably had no trouble with the first half—until you reached question 12. Most readers will likely find the answers to questions 12, 15, 16, 17, 19, 20, 21, 22, 23, 24, and 25 problematical. Now maybe you can see why so many people are having second thoughts about using the proof-text method of Bible study.

For many years I gave Bible studies to people interested in joining my church. In fact, when I went to the seminary during the late summer of 1964, I intended to do my M.A. major in New Testament studies. But my close friend and colleague Russell Burrill, who arrived at the seminary about three months ahead of me, convinced me that I should change my emphasis to systematic theology. Why? Because, he told me, that discipline would be most useful in my pastoral work when I prepared Bible studies to give to interested people and new converts. So I shifted mental gears and majored in systematic theology.

After graduating from the seminary and arriving at the churches in Massachusetts, I immediately set to work preparing my own Bible studies. I didn't want to rely on those "canned" studies that others—sometimes anonymous people—had prepared. My goal was to produce a set of Bible studies (and later a series of evangelistic sermons) that would scrupulously consider the context of the biblical passages I would array to prove my— no, the Bible's—points.

Old Testament Examples of Misguided Proof-texting

One of the texts I used—as did many other Bible instructors, pastors, and evangelists—was Ezekiel 18:20. It says, "The soul that sinneth, it shall die." What a great text to use when studying the state of the dead! As you know, the common misconception among many Christians is that whereas the body itself dies, the soul is immortal and survives death—either in heaven or hell or maybe purgatory.

Jesus said, however: "Fear him which is able to destroy both soul and body in hell" (Matt. 10:28). I used that sound bite from Ezekiel 18:20 to provide corroborative evidence that the soul is not inherently immortal but can indeed perish from hellfire.

Then one day as I was reading Ezekiel, I noticed the remaining words of Ezekiel 18:20 as well as the wider context. It shocked me. I had been misusing this biblical passage! The message that God had given to the prophet was not at all concerned about whether the soul vis à vis the body is or is not immortal. Had that been His concern, it would be what philosophers call an ontological statement—a description of one's inner essence, one's inner being. But there was nothing ontological about God's revelation to Ezekiel.

God's conversation with him was truly shocking in its own terms, though. Apparently a well-known proverb of Ezekiel's time said, "The fathers have eaten sour grapes, and the children's teeth are set on edge" (Eze. 18:2). The gist was that offspring suffer for what their forebears do. When parents eat unripe grapes, it doesn't affect them—just their off-spring.

This concept of deferred retribution appears even in the Decalogue: "I the Lord thy God am a jealous God, visiting the iniquity of the fathers upon the children unto the third and fourth generation of them that hate me" (Ex. 20:5). It was not just the next generation that would be punished for their forebears' sins; the punishment could extend to the grandchildren, to the great-grandchildren, and even to the great-great-grandchildren. (Also we need to keep in mind that biblical people lived in extended families that might include several generations at the same time. A house might have grandparents, grandchildren, and even great-grandchildren living in it simultaneously. They would have to share the consequences of the actions of any one of the multiple generations.)

"Don't believe it," God told Ezekiel. And the rest of chapter 18 contains variations on this radical new theme that punishment is reserved for the guilty party only, thereby turning the well-used adage on its head. The innocent will not suffer divine retribution in lieu of the party in the wrong. A good man "shall not die for the iniquity of his father, he shall surely live" (verse 17).

Now verse 20 in its entirety began to make sense to me: "The soul that sinneth, it shall die. The son shall not bear the iniquity of the father, neither shall the father bear the iniquity of the son: the righteousness of the righteous shall be upon him, and the wickedness of the wicked shall be upon him."

Syntactically the expression "it shall die" is emphatic and gets repeated in various ways (including its flipside) throughout chapter 18. "He shall surely live" (verse 9). "He shall surely die" (verse 13). "He shall surely live" (verse 17). "Even he shall die in his iniquity" (verse 18). "He shall surely live" (verse 21). "He shall live" (verse 22). "He shall surely live" (verse 28). "It shall die" is equivalent to saying "it *itself* shall die." In short, you will get what you deserve. And according to this chapter, it worked both ways. The unrighteous individual would receive from God his or her just deserts—"the soul that sinneth, it shall die." And the righteous person would receive from God his or her just deserts—"in his righteousness that he hath done he shall live" (verse 22).

The concept came as something scandalous to Ezekiel's readers. After all, they knew what God had said in the Ten Commandments, and they remembered that in Numbers 14:18 Moses had echoed God's declaration. Not only would Ezekiel's audience see this as contrary to God's Word written by the divine finger on tables of stone, but also they would feel that God had somehow offended their sensitivities by being unfair—or to use their terminology, *not equal.* "Yet ye say, The way of the Lord is not equal" (verse 25).

Of course, *their* response offends *our* modern-day sensitivities. In *our* understanding as Western individualists, we applaud the idea that guilt is privately owned and that people should suffer for their own misbehavior and not for the wrongful acts of others. But from their Eastern communal perspective, they reckoned that culpability is shared in community solidarity and that people deserved retribution for the sins of others in their kinship group and even in the population at large.

But their accusation boomeranged: "Hear now, O house of Israel," God said. "Is not my way equal? are not your ways unequal?" (verse 25). God was critiquing what they regarded as common sense. (It's not often that God's ideas match so closely our Western viewpoint.)

Here's another example of wrenching a sound bite—or proof-text—from its Old Testament setting.

I grew up in a pastor's home and am a product of my church's educational system from first grade through the seminary. Sometimes I began to feel like Samuel because I was in church so much of the time! My twin uncles were also pastors, and when our three families got together for Thanksgiving or for no special holiday at all, church shoptalk dominated the conversation. So immersed had I been in church activities—prayer meeting, Sabbath school, church services, vespers, Bible studies, evangelistic meetings, etc.—that I could sometimes (too often, I'm afraid) forget that context is essential to a correct understanding of Scripture. And so, I'm ashamed to admit it, I could use the proof-text method just like the best and the rest of them!

Two common themes in my church have been answered prayers and life in the earth made new. As early as cradle roll (now called beginners) and kindergarten, those of us raised in the church have heard that God eagerly responds to the prayer requests of boys and girls, and we've also been barraged with a volley of graphic metaphorical language describing what the new earth will be like.

One of our favorite sources for both emphases is Isaiah 65 and 66. And if the truth must be told, I've dipped into these two chapters for proof-texts more times than I care to disclose.

One of the passages that I cited again and again to encourage parishioners was Isaiah 65:24, which contains this sound bite: "Before they call, I will answer; and while they are yet speaking, I will hear." How many Christians, do you suppose, have taken from this verse abundant comfort for the here and now? God is so eager to answer our prayers that He responds before we've even finished our plea. In fact, He acts even before we make our request! So you, dear one suffering from cancer or you, cherished one hurting because of falling income and mounting debts, take heart. Say your prayers and look for God's answer, because He will respond even before the words roll off your tongue! This promise is for George Müller and for Roger Morneau and for you—yes, for you! Pray now! Watch for the answer now!

Isaiah 65:24 has comforted so many sufferers that I feel a bit reluctant to use it to finish our present discussion. But again, one day as I was reading my Bible, I did a double take when I read this scripture in its context. Now, don't jump to any conclusions! It is true that verse 24 is talking about prayer requests to God. Let's get that straight before proceeding further. The passage is about prayer—and answered prayer! But . . .

Why was I so startled when I read these cherished words from God? Because from verse 17 on down to verse 24 and then verse 25 following, the subject matter is what will take place when God creates "new heavens and a new earth" (verse 17). He was promising that what He was about to create would be radically different from what we experience in the here and now. (And don't forget that *that* here and now was not the twenty-first century but what Isaiah's audience knew way back there during the early 700s B.C.)

We find some startling yet appealing contrasts set forth, because "the former [heavens and earth] shall not be remembered, nor come into mind" (verse 17).

In the here and now weeping characterizes existence, but then "the voice of weeping shall be no more heard in her [Jerusalem]" (verse 19).

In the here and now children die in infancy (ever hear of SIDS or other dreadful illnesses that kill newborns and even toddlers?), but then "the child shall die an hundred years old" (verse 20).

In the here and now people lose their comfortable homes in foreclosure, but then "they shall build houses, and inhabit them" (verse 21).

In the here and now truck farmers and even backyard farmers lose crops to drought or disease or insect infestation, but then "they shall plant vineyards, and eat the fruit of them" (verse 21).

In the here and now eventually old age turns vigor into feebleness, sure footsteps into tottering ones, and we celebrate at funerals those lives no longer with us, but then "as the days of a tree are the days of my people" (verse 22).

In the here and now wolves prey upon livestock (just ask the ranchers near Yellowstone National Park who have had animals killed and eaten by the wolves reintroduced into that environment), but then "the wolf and the lamb shall feed together" (verse 25).

In the here and now African lions and New World mountain lions slaughter other forms of wildlife (sometimes even humans), but then "the lion shall eat straw like the bullock" (verse 25).

In the here and now cobras, Gaboon vipers, Taipans, and other poisonous snakes envenomate smaller species of animals and swallow them whole, but then "dust shall be the serpent's meat [food]" (verse 25).

And in the here and now sincere prayers go unanswered and we talk about the mysterious "silence of God" (as did the psalmist and some of the prophets), but then "before they call, I will answer; and while they are yet speaking, I will hear" (verse 24).

God's astounding promise to hear prayers so quickly that the answer comes before we can even say amen is what will happen *in the world to come*. He's not speaking at all about the here and now. (Yes, God sometimes has answers forming to our prayers before we utter them, but it is the exception rather than the rule.)

We also learn something else about future bliss in Isaiah 65 and 66. In those chapters death will still mar human existence. The corpses of God's enemies will lie rotting and stinking outside Jerusalem, and His people "shall go forth, and look upon the carcasses of the men that have transgressed against me: for their worm shall not die, neither shall their fire be quenched; and they shall be an abhorring unto all flesh" (Isa. 66:24). And God's own people won't be exempt from death, but there will be no premature death there. That's what the words "the child shall die an hundred years old" (Isa. 65:20) mean. A 100-year-old child is an oxymoron—like jumbo shrimp or saying nothing or unborn children or interstate highways in Hawaii. You get the picture. There will be death "then," but it will never be premature. (We need to go to the New Testament to learn that in the earth made new there will be no death.)

New Testament Examples of Misguided Proof-texting

We could consider additional Old Testament examples, but now let's turn to two examples from the New Testament of proof-texting gone wrong.

Since we just finished talking about the world to come as described in Isaiah 65 and 66, let's examine a passage from Paul that many use (yes, I must plead guilty once again) as a sound bite to describe the wonders of the world to come. Here's the passage in question: "Eye hath not seen, nor ear heard, neither have entered into the heart of man, the things which God hath prepared for them that love him" (1 Cor. 2:9).

If you're like me, you can't even begin to count the number of times you've heard that verse used with the intent that it will put everyone in awe of the unimaginable world to come—in heaven and on the new earth. It's a great sound bite, a helpful proof-text, to wow us into believing that the future that God has planned for us exceeds our highest expectations . . . *if* that is indeed what Paul is talking about.

Please forgive me if I sound like a grumpy grouch who delights in bursting bubbles. In fact, it pains me to inform you that the world to come was not even on the apostle's horizon when he penned those words. Really.

Interestingly, he was citing the prophet Isaiah—and probably out of context at that. (See Isa. 64:4.) But we won't let that sidetrack our current discussion. (First-century Jews habitually cited individual scriptural passages out of context in their theological discussions. They didn't have the awareness and sensitivity that we have when it comes to the importance of context.)

If Paul wasn't talking about heaven (and/or the new earth), what was his intent when he quoted (a bit freely) Isaiah 64:4? We should begin our quest for understanding with verse 1, in which the apostle assures the Corinthian church members that when he evangelized them he didn't try to impress them with wisdom and fancy words. He said that he had one goal only. "I determined not to know any thing among you, save Jesus Christ, and him crucified" (1 Cor. 2:2). The "wise" approaches that the "world" might take didn't taint his presentation.

Instead of utilizing the wisdom of this world, Paul presented the wisdom of God. However, "none of the princes of this world knew" (verse 8) this wisdom that was hidden in (and maybe by) God Himself. If they'd had a clue as to who Jesus was, "they would not have crucified the Lord of glory" (verse 8).

What I find so interesting here is that Paul, who could at times be so hard-hitting, in this letter to the Corinthian believers is presenting an excuse—a kind of alibi, if you will—for the behavior of those responsible for the Crucifixion. Paul is not blaming them for their cruel actions, because they were ignorant of who Jesus really was.

They just didn't know, and Isaiah foretold this lack of knowledge when he quoted Paul as writing that "eye hath not seen, nor ear heard, neither have entered into the heart of man, the things which God hath prepared for them that love him" (verse 9). Jesus was among "the things which God hath prepared for them that love him," but His contemporaries didn't have a clue. And so they crucified Jesus. But if they had known, "they would not have crucified the Lord of glory" (verse 8).

Paul didn't stop there, though, with the excuse for the rulers of this world. They may indeed have been ignorant of who Jesus was, "but God hath revealed them unto us by his Spirit: for the Spirit searcheth all things, yea, the deep things of God" (verse 10). And these hidden mysteries are those "things [which] also we speak, not in the words which man's wisdom teacheth, but which the Holy Ghost teacheth; comparing spiritual things with spiritual" (verse 13).

Finally, Paul clinches his line of argumentation with these words: "For who hath known the mind of the Lord, that he may instruct him? But we have the mind of Christ" (verse 16). The apostle contrasted the world leaders blissfully ignorant of God's preparations in Jesus Christ for our salvation with the apostles and even the Corinthian Christians who had learned spiritual secrets from the Holy Spirit!

OK, let's look at one more favorite proof-text that we typically wrench from its context, making it say something quite different from what the inspired New Testament writer meant to say. The passage in question is 2 Timothy 3:16, which declares: "All scripture is given by inspiration of God."

Oh, how many evangelists and Bible instructors have loved this sound bite from the apostle Paul! Whenever the authority of Scripture comes up, they repeat this snippet of Pauline counsel to Timothy: "All scripture is given by inspiration of God. . . . All scripture is given by inspiration of God. . . . All scripture is given by inspiration of God."

Why am I using this as an example of a scriptural sound bite gone wrong? Let me explain by first talking about the grammar, then the vocabulary, and finally the context itself.

First, here's the necessary information about the *grammar*. Second Timothy 3:16 lacks a verb. If you look in your King James Version, you'll likely see that the word "is" appears twice in the text—in italics. When we want to emphasize something today, we use italics so that the word stands out. That's not the reason that italics appear in the KJV, however. Whenever you see a word in italic face in the KJV, that means the italicized word is not in the original Hebrew or Greek text but has been supplied by the translators.

One of the first things a student of the Greek language learns is that forms of the verb "to be" are often implied in the text though not used. That means, for instance, the Greek word for "is" had been omitted. Anyone who knows Greek doesn't find this troubling and simply supplies the English word "is" in the proper place. Not a big deal—it's part of Greek grammar, as it is in a number of other languages.

But in 2 Timothy 3:16 scholars face the problem of where to place the supplied "is." The KJV puts it in two places: "All scripture [1] *is* given by inspiration . . . and [2] *is* profitable for . . ." That's appropriate and not wrong. However, the translator need not supply the word "is" twice. Just once would suffice, and the text could read either: "All scripture given by inspiration of God *is* profitable for . . ." or "All scripture *is* given by inspiration of God and profitable for . . ."

The former rendition appears in a number of translations. Here are a few. "Every holy Writing which comes from God is of profit for . . ." (Basic English). "Everything that is written under divine inspiration is helpful for . . ." (TCNT). "Every inspired scripture has its use for . . ." (NEB). The sense is that whatever scriptures God has inspired are truly profitable. This, of course, allows readers to infer that not all scriptures are inspired, but those that are will be beneficial. Such a translation does not do violence to the grammar of the text. It is a possible way of rendering Paul's instruction to Timothy. The question we need to ask is this: Even though this rendition is grammatically *possible*, is it contextually *probable*? Obviously, some translators thought that it was indeed probable, but the majority of versions disagree and opt for the latter translation.

Maybe the *vocabulary* that Paul employed can help us decide between the two grammatical options. We could say a lot about each word the apostle used, but we'll briefly discuss just two of them.

The first word I'd like to call your attention to is the Greek adjective *theopneustos*, which the KJV renders as "given by inspiration of God"—five words to translate one adjective. Paul used a compound word here, which literally means "God-breathed." The apostle didn't make up the term, although it appears only this one time in the New Testament. A few non-biblical Greek documents (*Sentences of Pseudo-Phocylides* 121; *Sybylline Oracles* 5. 308, 406) used it to describe the state a seer would enter when receiving oracles. It appears to have been a synonym for the Greek term from which we get the English word "enthusiasm."

The concept behind the word is that God is somehow active. Does He breathe life *into something* or does He breathe *upon someone*? When I see the word *theopneustos*, my thoughts immediately go back to when God sculpted the first man from the earth and breathed the breath of life into his nostrils, causing Adam to come to life. Paul uses the word to describe

Scripture, but understanding the etymology of the term doesn't really help us decide whether Paul has in mind *either* that all Scripture is God-breathed and profitable *or* whether he meant that all God-breathed Scripture is profitable.

The other vocabulary term we should briefly consider is *graphï*, the Greek word here translated "Scripture." The word literally refers to what is written and so can legitimately be translated "writing." In fact, in the Septuagint version of Daniel 5:17 we read that Daniel told King Balshazzar, "I will read the writing." Daniel was, of course, referring to the handwriting on the wall, which technically speaking wasn't Scripture, though it was apparent that God was behind it. The Greek term *graphï* didn't *necessarily* refer to biblical scriptures. It could denote anything written.

So was Paul saying that all writing was inspired—God-breathed? The fact is that in the ancient Near East people considered the art of writing a gift from the gods.

The Egyptians believed that the goddess Seshat invented writing, then the god Thoth shared it with humanity. Ultimately Thoth came to be seen as the originator of writing. Interestingly, the Egyptian method of writing is called "hieroglyphics," or sacred writing.

In Mesopotamia the Sumerians had a legend that said the god Enki taught this divine skill to earthlings. The Babylonians, who lived much later than the Sumerians, thought that the god Nabu, son of Marduk and Enki's grandson, developed writing and passed this blessing along to human beings.

But it hardly seems possible that Paul believed that writing in general—all writing—was a divine gift and that he therefore said that whatever gets written is God-breathed. And although *graphï* could refer to writing other than Scripture (and indeed, the Greek of Daniel 5:17 did use it that way), the term appears many times in the New Testament, each time as a synonym of "Bible."

So we don't find any helpful hints in the vocabulary that Paul used—at least clues that would help us decide whether he meant "All scripture given by inspiration of God *is* profitable for . . ." or "All scripture *is* given by inspiration of God and profitable for . . . ."

But before we leave our limited discussion about Paul's vocabulary, we should be aware of one other word Paul employed—*kai*. Most commonly we translate this Greek word as "and," but it can also mean "that is," "even," or "also." And Paul inserted that word *kai* between the Greek words translated "inspired/God-breathed" and "profitable/useful." This position of *kai* makes it a bit awkward to translate Paul's words as "All scripture given by inspiration of God *is* profitable for . . ." If that is indeed what Paul intended, he could have left out the word *kai*. So the presence of that conjunction seems to tilt us in favor of the more common translation "All scripture *is* given by inspiration of God and profitable for . . ."

It's time now to turn to the *context* of 2 Timothy 3:16. And here we come to a surprising conclusion. All that argument over whether Paul meant "All scripture given by inspiration of God *is* profitable for . . ." or "All scripture *is* given by inspiration of God and profitable for . . ." is really a tempest in a teapot. It misses entirely the point Paul makes here to young Timothy.

Luke Timothy Johnson points out that "the debate is not central to Paul's point" (*Anchor Bible for the First and Second Letters to Timothy*, vol. 35A, p. 420). The apostle was not trying to drum into Timothy's mind that the Bible—all Scripture—is inspired. Nor was Paul here acting as an apologist or an evangelist trying to convince a nonbeliever that Scripture, namely the Old Testament, was a product of divine inspiration.

Rather Paul was encouraging Timothy to read his Bible, because it is profitable to do so. The apostle did not have in mind monetary gain here. The term translated "profitable" in the KJV means "helpful." Then Paul delineates four ways that Scripture is useful.

First, the Sacred Word is "profitable for doctrine." The Greek word that the KJV translates as "doctrine" means "teaching." The Greek word for teachers was *didaskalos*, and what they transmitted to their students was *didaskalian*. The act of teaching was of utmost importance in the early Christian church, and Paul refers to teachers again and again—even within the book of 2 Timothy.

One of the spiritual gifts that Paul listed in his Epistle to the Ephesian Christians was teaching. "And he gave some, apostles; and some, prophets; and some, evangelists; and some, pastors and teachers" (Eph. 4:11). The syntax of this passage indicates that the last gift mentioned in verse 11 is a single gift—pastor-teacher.

If Timothy had received the spiritual gift of being a pastor (shepherd)-teacher, then the Bible was certainly most useful for him, and he should spend much time reading and contemplating it. Scripture—yes, inspired scripture—would be profitable to Timothy in his role as teacher.

Second, Paul said that Scripture "is profitable for . . . reproof." We could also translate the term as "rebuking" or "refuting error." The various families of New Testament Greek manuscripts use either of two words here: *elenchon*, found in Codex Bezae and the Koine tradition, or, *elegmon*, supported by codices Alexandrinus and Sinaiticus and many other manuscripts. How did this use of two different words occur? Most likely by one of two possible ways: (1) faulty hearing—misunderstanding what had been read aloud; or (2) faulty handwriting—sloppily writing the word in question and thereby making it ambiguous to the next scribe.

The two words have similar though not quite identical meanings. The latter term appears often in the Septuagint (the Greek translation of the Old Testament, often referred to by the abbreviation LXX), where it means punishment. The first was almost a technical word used in discussions about logic. It had the sense of proving a point, although on rare occasions it could connote reproof, which is related to punishment.

As a leader of the early church, Timothy needed the skills of logically proving a point as well as of disciplining errant church members. By reading his Bible he would find help in doing these two distinct, though sometimes related, activities.

Third, the apostle affirmed that Timothy would find Scripture "profitable for . . . correction." The sense behind the word Paul chose to use is that of setting something right, "especially in the moral sense" (*ibid.*, p. 421). Paul's choice of vocabulary here has the connotation of improvement. Reading the Old Testament would help Timothy personally in his moral growth, and he in turn would be able to aid others in their ethical and spiritual odyssey.

Fourth, Paul told Timothy that by paying attention to God's Word, he would gain an education in righteousness, because it "is profitable for . . . instruction in righteousness." The apostle used the noun *paideía* here, which means training or nurture or discipline. It could denote both the act (the cause) of upbringing and its result (the effect).

But the apostle had in mind a special training course. Scripture is profitable for educating someone in righteousness. The Greek noun *dikaiosúnï* comes from the root word *dikï*, which means the right way, the proper direction, that which was culturally acceptable. In the Bible the word refers to the lifestyle that God expects of His people, the way of life that receives His seal of approval.

By studying Scripture Timothy would gain an education in how to live right, how to behave so that he would receive God's approbation. "Scripture serves as a source of moral and spiritual improvement. This is made clear by the final, summative statement of function: Scripture is useful for an entire education in righteousness" (*ibid.*, p. 424).

Now perhaps you can understand why I feel that using 2 Timothy 3:16 as a sound bite to demonstrate the inspiration of the Bible is off-base. The topic of utmost concern in Paul's mind is not how inspired God's Word is and what the process of inspiration involves. Rather, the point the apostle is making to his young protégé is that the inspired corpus is practical in four distinct ways, which he proceeds to spell out. "Paul's purpose in talking about Scripture is to make a point about its usefulness. Therefore 3:16-17 is not an ontological but a functional statement" (*ibid.*, p. 423).

In Summation

We could examine other instances of proof-texting gone awry, but the preceding examples should suffice. From them I hope that you've gained new insights into the passages we explored. But more than that, I also hope that now you can see how misleading sound bites from Scripture can be when quoted or used in isolation.

Furthermore, from my own personal experience I can testify that curing this misuse of God's Word can be very difficult to do. Many of us have become so accustomed to the proof-text method that it can be very difficult to see its dangers and to break the habit of using sound bites from the Bible to prove a point that the inspired writers didn't even have in mind.

It boils down to developing "a very high degree of journalistic ethics." Once we have cultivated this sensitivity, then we must take our study of Scripture seriously, looking at the context before and after each proof-text that we may be tempted to use. It is appropriate for us to learn how to rightly divide the word of truth (2 Tim. 2:15). This may be difficult to do, but it's worth it. Try it yourself, and get ready for the surprises . . . and blessings . . . that it will bring to you.

CHAPTER 4

Cultural Norms— Shame and Honor

When my own denomination sent its first missionary overseas, it didn't have much concern about giving him some orientation and sensitivity training before he landed on a foreign shore. The man and his family simply boarded a rickety ship and, you can be sure, spent some very uncomfortable days crossing the Atlantic Ocean. Fortunately, he was sailing only to Europe. So culture shock was relatively minimal for him.

But later more missionaries left the shores of America. They went to South America and worked among Indian tribes there. Others headed for Africa and India and Egypt and China and the South Sea Islands. Those courageous missionaries experienced the depths of culture shock. It wasn't just a matter of learning a different language, although that can be truly daunting. Other cultural changes were perplexing and even challenging: what one ate, how one ate, when one ate, where one ate, and with whom one ate; what one wore (or didn't wear); how one treated (or mistreated) others; what was considered polite (and what was rude); how one adorned (or disfigured) one's body; whom one married (or couldn't marry); what body parts could be uncovered (or should be covered).

Examples of Cultural Norms

In the United States stealing includes picking up a child's toy from a sidewalk and walking away with it. The people of Mexico do not consider that a crime. In Bible times one could pick fruit without impunity from an orchard while walking through it. Don't try that in the United States! In the English language repeating a word indicates emphasis, as in "he is very very small," meaning someone quite tiny. However, in the Hiligaynon language spoken in the Philippines, repeating a word lessens its significance, so in the example above the person would be fairly large. When we talk about someone having a big heart, we mean that the individual is generous. However, the Shilluk people of the Anglo-Egyptian Sudan call someone who is stingy bighearted. Yet the Akha people of Myanmar think that someone who has a big heart is egotistical.

Did you know that in a number of cultures in-laws have nothing to do with one another? In certain parts of Africa, people avoid attending Christian weddings because they know they'll be expected to greet in-laws, thereby crossing—and violating—kinship lines. In America once upon a time—maybe even today in some situations—a Navajo man would never speak directly to his mother-in-law. If he wanted to say something to her, he had to use a go-between.

The only universal no-nos that anthropologists have discovered are murder and incest. Every society known has sanctions against them. However, the definition of murder and incest can vary widely from culture to culture.

In some societies murder refers to killing only certain people—those considered part of the in group. It may be abhorrent if one kills a fellow tribe member, but killing someone outside the group may be laudatory. Few cultures rarely, if ever, equate every taking of human life with murder. In the Ten Commandments it is murder that is forbidden, and not just all kinds of killing (Ex. 20:13). That's why God could proscribe murder in the Decalogue but tell the ancient Israelites to kill every man, woman, and child (and even all of the animals) of their enemies (Deut. 25:19; 1 Sam. 15:3; Deut. 7:1, 2; 20:17; compare Joshua 6:21; 11:11).

Incest refers to having sexual intercourse with those considered close kin. For instance, the Nuer people of the Anglo-Egyptian Sudan regard having sexual relations with anyone of the same clan to be incest. But in the Old Testament, Abraham sent his servant to find a wife for Isaac from the clan back in Mesopotamia (Gen. 24:1-4). If a Tonga man in Mozambique is about to go hunting hippopotami, he is expected to engage in sex with his daughter, which his culture does not consider as incest. And the Mosaic laws command Levirate marriage, in which a man's brother was obligated to have sex with his sister-in-law if his brother died and left the wife childless (Deut. 25:5-10).

Before my church sends out missionaries today, the new recruits attend predeparture mission institutes conducted by the Institute of World Mission. These seminars help the missionaries-to-be to understand cultural differences. Yet even after these intensive sessions to sensitize the prospective missionaries to different ways of looking at things, once expatriates arrive at their destination, cultural shock can still be nearly overwhelming.

Examples of Cultural Norms in the Ancient Near East

Just as we are ignorant of the cultural mores of modern societies other than ours, so most of us have little or no idea of the cultural milieu of the biblical society of the ancient Near East. When we read in the Bible about the actions and words of biblical characters—be they heroes or villains—we tend to interpret what we read in terms of our own Western viewpoints, unaware that the ancient Near Eastern world was vastly different culturally from our society.

It's understandable that we do this. Culture tends to be something most of us take for granted. Having been raised in it, we assume that its practices constitute the only "natural" way of doing something. We're no more aware of most of our cultural behaviors than we are of the air pressure around us. And so it can be quite disturbing to encounter another culture and discover that the customs we take for granted are hardly universally accepted.

For example, when Western government officials first went to Sudan, they became incensed when the Shilluk leaders remained seated when they, the British, entered the room. Why were they being treated with such disrespect? Then the Western administrators learned that among the Shilluk people standing in the presence of someone else showed disrespect and contempt, whereas sitting demonstrated deference and esteem.

Similarly, when we open the Bible, we are entering a world quite unlike ours. The cultural assumptions people "back then" made (and lived by) often differed greatly from those we follow. So we can very easily misunderstand the dynamics going on within the scriptural accounts.

Many people in the ancient Near East were deeply troubled by the concept of the "evil eye." And they weren't talking about being nearsighted or farsighted or having cataracts—even though eye disease was common back then. (In fact, the city of Laodicea had become famous for the eye medicine concocted there—*kollúrion*, often translated as "eyesalve" [Rev. 3:18].) What, then, was the evil eye that people so much feared?

If we wish to understand what the evil eye involved, first we must learn that during the first century people believed that the eye was like a flashlight, throwing light onto what the individual looked at. In fact, many thought that the heart was the source of this light, which was then transmitted through the eyes to illuminate what was "out there."

If a person had a good heart, then the light that the heart generated was benevolent. And when that good light shone upon those whom the good-hearted person focused on, then it blessed the person being looked at. However, if people had an evil heart, then the light that their corrupt heart generated was malevolent. And when that evil-hearted individual stared at someone else, that evil light would hurt the person being gazed upon. But the benevolent light shining from the eyes of generous people would produce beneficial results in the lives of others. And if avaricious persons gazed at someone else, the evil light shining from their evil eyes would cause disastrous effects.

In overly simplistic terms, the evil eye was often a covetous eye, which would lead to ill effects in the lives of others. "In this way generous persons can look on others and do actual good, while envious persons can look on others and do real damage. . . . Genuine fear of the evil eye was a constant concern to Jesus' hearers" (Richard Rohrbaugh, *The Social Sciences and New Testament Interpretation*, p. 4).

Now read what Jesus said in Matthew 6:22, 23: "The light of the body is the eye: if therefore thine eye be single, thy whole body shall be full of light. But if thine eye be evil, thy whole body shall be full of darkness. If therefore the light that is in thee be darkness, how great is that darkness!" Do you understand this passage differently now that you've read the previous few paragraphs?

"No biblical writer had modern Americans in mind when he wrote. . . . Few Americans have ancient Palestinian peasants in mind when they read the Bible. . . . . Now social-science critics . . . have begun to realize the magnitude of the *social* distance between the [New Testament] and ourselves" (*ibid.*, pp. 1, 2).

How, then, when we read the Bible can we look outside our own culture and peer inside that of the ancient Near East? If we don't somehow become able to do this, we're going to misunderstand a lot of what we encounter in Scripture.

Thankfully, there's a relatively new discipline called "social-science criticism" that is gaining in popularity among biblical scholars. This discipline, as with the other forms of biblical criticism, is not necessarily negative in connotation. It is, rather, an academic approach that helps us understand the dynamics within the ancient Middle Eastern culture(s).

Richard L. Rohrbaugh is considered one of the founders of social-science criticism of religious texts. Other prominent scholars in the field include Bruce J. Malina, Jerome H. Neyrey, John H. Elliott, Halvor Moxnes, Douglas E. Oakman, and Lucretia B. Yaghjian. The idea behind social-science criticism is to interpret the biblical writings in their original cultural context. By so doing, we gain insight into why people did and said what we find in the Bible. It can help us read the Bible on its own terms and more clearly grasp its concepts and teachings.

"Historical criticism concentrates on events, while literary criticism concentrates on literary texts. Social-scientific criticism concentrates on social structures, processes, and interactions. Theological criticism concentrates on religious and dogmatic belief and practice" (John H. Elliott, *What Is Social-science Criticism?* p. 90). "So Social science criticism helps us to understand why things were done" (www.aboutthebible.com).

And it could be a fatal flaw for us as Bible students to read into the activities and conversations of the biblical texts *our* understanding of what those behaviors mean. The most natural thing in the world is for us to view the Bible through the glasses of Western American culture, but natural though it may be, it can mislead us. "If the culture of the original is at any given point very similar to ours, our reflexes are going to serve us fairly well. . . . Such a situation is rarely the case between Euro-American culture and the Hebrew and Aramaic portions of the Scripture. . . . The amount of biblical material where there is such close cultural similarity to our agreements is, however, distressingly small" (Charles H. Kraft, *Christianity in Culture*, p. 133).

"We, as readers, may not understand major portions of what is going on at all, since we don't know the cultural agreements. In the story of the woman at the well, for example, we are likely to miss entirely the significance of such things as Jesus' going through Samaria, his talking to a woman, the fact that the woman was at the well at midday, the necessity that she go back to get her supposed husband before she could make a decision, etc. For us to understand such things we need large doses of explanation by those who study the cultural background" (*ibid.*, p. 132).

Of course, not all of us can be social-science authorities. However, we can benefit from its research by reading what the experts have written. While I do not pretend to be an expert in the discipline, in the rest of this chapter and several following it I'll share with you some of the insights I've learned from social-science investigations of Scripture. I hope you'll find the material as helpful as I have. For me it has opened many windows that illuminate the dynamics of what is going on just beneath the surface of the scriptural accounts.

The Dyadic Personality

Perhaps one of the first things that we should learn about is what social-science critics call the "dyadic personality." It's not a terribly difficult concept to get the mind around—even for us individualistic Westerners. The fact is that much of the world today—probably 70 percent—consists of people with dyadic personalities. It's basically Western Europeans and Americans who are the exceptions to this mind-set. Did you know that the concept of individualism really didn't come into vogue (in Western societies) until the sixteenth century? Up to then pretty much all cultures were not individualistic but collectivistic in perspective. The importance of the group as a whole superseded that of the individual person.

In America you'll often hear someone say, "I don't care what other people think. I'm going to do . . ." Such an expression is symptomatic of Western individualism. Wasn't it Frank Sinatra who sang the song "My Way"? We're going to be self-sufficient, and we don't need our neighbors' help. In fact, we really don't much care what our neighbors think about us. (We may not even know their names.) But that's not the perspective of most people in the world, who have dyadic personalities.

Merriam-Webster's Collegiate Dictionary (11th edition) defines "dyadic" as "two individuals . . . maintaining a sociologically significant relationship." People with dyadic personalities see themselves not as individuals standing alone but as persons whose identity comes from their interaction with others. If I have a dyadic personality, then in order to know "who I am" I must look to other people.

Here's a definition I found on the Internet. Dyadic personalities "internalize and make their own what others say, do, and think about them, because they believe it is necessary, for being human, to live out the expectations of others. These persons conceive of themselves as always interrelated to other persons while occupying a distinct social position both horizontally (with others sharing the same status, moving from center to periphery) and vertically (with others above and below in social rank). Such persons need to test this interrelatedness, with the focus of attention away from ego, on the demands and expectations of others who can grant or withhold reputation."

In short, the self-image of a dyadic personality depends on what others think about that person. Such people are said to be "embedded" in the other people of their society. A dyadic personality always needs to know what others think—think about him or her specifically. That's how one achieves his or her self-identity. "Codependency is the desired outcome of child rearing" in dyadic societies (Rohrbaugh, p. 48). Dyadic personalities "need other people to continue to know who they really are" (*ibid.*).

Americans belong to what social-science critics call "weak group society." We see ourselves as personally and individually responsible for who we are and what we do. The idea that "I am the master of my fate" comes from a "weak group." People in the ancient Near East—along with most people in the world today—belong to a "strong group" society. Every person's identity is tied to the group within which he or she is raised and how that group perceives him or her.

Dyadic personalities "always feel themselves as embedded in a group, as representatives of the group, as needing others to know who they are and what they are doing. . . . The individual does not primarily perceive himself or herself as unique but as a group member. Group belonging and group location is primary and essential to self-definition. . . . The individual would feel responsible, for the most part, to the group (not to the self) for his or her own actions, destiny, career, development, and life in general" (Bruce J. Malina, *Christian Origins and Cultural Anthropology*, p. 19). In such cultures people define who they are by the family, clan, tribe, village, nation, religion, profession, or social and economic level they belong to. They will not just tell you that they are Joe or Sue, but Joe or Sue, son or daughter of Henry the shoemaker.

So when you read about the people featured in Scripture, you must understand their behavior—words and actions (both denoted by the same Hebrew word: *dabar*)—in terms of their having a dyadic personality, because they were embedded in a strong group. Perhaps one of the most interesting examples of this for Christians is Jesus' questions to His disciples: "Whom do men say that I am?" and "Whom say ye that I am?" (Mark 8:27, 29). Most of the time, though, Jesus' self-image was a reality because of how His heavenly Father viewed Him.

Pilate offers another example of a dyadic personality. At the trial of Jesus, the Roman official found himself torn between what his wife thought of him, who Jesus Himself claimed to be and His lack of reaction to Pilate, what the Jewish religious leaders (probably mostly Sadducees) wanted, what the shouting crowd said to him, and especially what Caesar thought of him. Pilate's self-image mirrored what others thought of him at that particular moment.

Honor and Shame

As a consequence of the dyadic personality dynamic of a strong group, honor was a vitally important value in the ancient Near East. And the concept of shame (the polar opposite of honor) similarly drove a person's behavior. "The culture of the first-century was built on the foundational social values of honor and dishonor" (David A. deSilva, *Honor, Patronage, Kinship, & Purity*, p. 23). "Honor and shame were pivotal values in antiquity that structured the daily lives of peoples around the Mediterranean" (Jerome H. Neyrey, *Honor and Shame in the Gospel of Matthew*, p. 3).

The ancient Near East was what is called a "limited goods society." People regarded the world as having only a finite supply of money, property, and even honor. There was barely enough to go around, so to speak. So if a person gained wealth or status, most likely someone else lost the same. "Saving face" is the name of this dynamic in many Asian societies.

But exactly what did honor consist of? It included one's standing both horizontally and vertically within society, as well as one's material wealth. But especially it consisted of how valuable others saw another person within society. So honor is a partial synonym for prestige and reputation. One had a certain right to honor. "Honor is a sentiment of worth felt by an individual, which is *claimed* before others and subsequently *acknowledged* by them" (Neyrey, p. 15).

One obtained honor by two basic methods: (a) by being born with it (called "ascribed honor"); or (b) by acquiring it (sometimes referred to as "achieved honor").

One had ascribed honor by virtue of the family origin. No one earned ascribed honor. It was something of a birthright. This is why the biblical world regarded genealogical information as very important. Also one's birth ranking within the family could determine the amount of ascribed honor he or she had. Firstborn children had more ascribed honor than their siblings, and so they inherited the larger share of their father's property. In addition, one's sex determined the amount of ascribed honor one had. Sons enjoyed more ascribed honor than daughters did. (Society viewed daughters as a potential source of dishonor for the family.)

One got achieved honor by one's behavior and by the expressed opinions of others. A soldier could gain honor by his brave feats in warfare. The victorious song of the women that "Saul hath slain his thousands, and David his ten thousands" (1 Sam. 18:7) is an example of David's achieved honor. He didn't have a lot of ascribed honor, being Jesse's last-born son. Besides, he was a shepherd, and many Jews held shepherds in disdain. But David's military prowess earned him honor. (By the same token, King Saul lost honor—gained shame—by what the women sang. David could gain honor only at Saul's expense.)

This honor/shame dynamic helps explain why in Greek—and later in Roman—society the encomium was so important. *Encomium* is a Greek term that in general referred to the praise of a person, a thing, or even an event. In rhetoric the encomium speech followed certain rules by which an orator formally paid tribute to someone else. The first step was to speak about where and how the hero was born, including his splendid forebears. Next, the person giving it would address the education and training that the subject had received. In the third part, the orator would go into detail about the hero's actions—what he had said and what he had done—emphasizing the virtues that he exemplified. Fourth, he would make comparisons that would put the recipient of the encomium in a favorable light.

Finally, the orator would end with some sort of epilogue, which (if the hero had died) would glorify the person's noble death.

Clearly, when an orator praised someone in an encomium, that person received—achieved—even more honor. Praising another was of great importance in a dyadic society, in which honor and shame were foundational notions. (In fact, there were many other ways to formally praise another person. The *panegyric, eulogy* [not for just those deceased], *epinicion, epithalamium,* and *prothalamion* were other forms of lauding others and thereby increasing their honor.)

Perhaps the most extravagant way of giving honor to another person was by proclaiming him to be divine—a common practice in the ancient Near East for kings, pharaohs, and emperors (although other humans could also be considered divine—as were Paul and Barnabas [Acts 14:11, 12]). Sometimes the ruler would assert it for himself, which would be a kind of ascribed honor because the king would claim some sort of special parentage. Other times the ruler would receive this distinction from those he ruled. Such an attribution might occur during the ruler's lifetime, and sometimes it was awarded after their death.

In the ancient Mesopotamian nation of Sumer, King Naram-Sin (who lived during the 2000s B.C.) appears to have been the first Mesopotamian king who claimed to be divine. Earlier than that, around 3100 B.C., Egyptian society considered Pharaoh Narmer divine, and from the Old Kingdom (c. 2686 –2181 B.C.) onward, people regularly regarded the pharaohs as gods. In first-century Rome many viewed the emperors as divine. Tiberius Caesar was known as "the August God, the son of the God Augustus" and "the grandson of the God Julius."

Obviously, calling rulers "divine" was not an ontological assertion—a claim such as we make when we say that YHWH is omnipotent (all-powerful), omniscient (all-wise), omnipresent (everywhere present), eternal, holy, etc. The constituents of the realm knew the foibles of their king. It was, rather, a way of attributing honor to the ruler—or a way that the ruler could ascribe honor to himself. To call another human being divine was the most definitive way of granting honor to another.

In the Semitic world of the Bible the expression "son of . . ." meant that the person so denominated had the qualities of the final word used. For instance, if you were "son of the day," you would have some of the characteristics of daytime—being full of light and goodness. And if others called you "son of hair," it would indicate you were hairy. When God referred to Ezekiel as "son of man" (Eze. 2:1, 3, 6, 8; 3:1, 3, 4, 10, 17, 25; 4:1, 16; etc.), He meant that Ezekiel was a typical human being. So to call another human being "son of God" was a Semitic way of saying that the individual person-ified (at least some of) the attributes that God Himself enjoyed. Since God exhibited creative power as well as controlling power, someone showing similar qualities could be honored by being called "son of God."

Having honor was like having a bank account of status. It could be added to and subtracted from. When people's bank accounts of repute re-ceived deposits, they enjoyed more honor. But withdrawals caused them to suffer shame. Because this was a patriarchal society, most of the honor was held in deposit for the males. The men strove to maintain a bank ac-count full of ever-increasing honor—being honor-full. A female, how-ever, was honorable if she was shame-full—deferring to a man by letting him precede her into a building, leaving a building ahead of a man, wear-ing a veil when in public view, and otherwise fulfilling the roles society expected of a "good girl"—to use a modern expression. For a woman, being shameful increased her honor, whereas being shameless decreased her honor.

Women were "expected to display shyness, not concern for prestige; deference, not concern for precedence; submission, not aggressiveness; timidity, not daring; and restraint, not boldness. . . . Females have 'honor' when they have this kind of 'shame'" (Neyrey, p. 32).

Since men spent most of their time outside the home—in the public eye—they were always alert for challenges to their honor, because other men were always ready and willing to increase their own personal bank ac-count of honor by shaming another man publicly. A whole set of rules de-fined how a male could defend his own honor while trying to detract from someone else's honor. Anthropologists refer to such a society as "agonis-tic," which means that the culture was rife with competition and aggres-siveness. It revealed itself on a national level in the constant warfare between nations and on an individual level in what social scientists refer to as "challenge and riposte."

A male had to learn the fine art of challenging his peers (a push, if you will), who would in turn respond with a riposte (a shove back, so to speak). It was honorable for peers—men with nearly equal amounts of honor in their bank account—to play this game of challenge and riposte. But biblical society did not approve of a man reacting to the challenge of another male with much less honor in his personal bank account of reputation. So a person needed to decide whether or not he could worthily respond to a challenge with a riposte. Sometimes the honorable thing to do was to ignore it. Furthermore, since honor was something one's peers projected onto the receptor, such verbal jousts had to be conducted in public.

The game generally consisted of four distinct steps: (1) a claim of honor, (2) a challenge to that claim, (3) a defense—riposte—of that claim, and (4) a public acclamation as to who gained honor and who lost it. If someone with a mere subsistence level of honor challenged a man who enjoyed much honor, the honorable thing to do was to punish him rather than engaging him with a riposte. In other words, to be challenged by someone else meant that the person doing the challenging was acknowledging the worth of the person he was verbally accosting. So when two men engaged in the game of challenge and riposte, they were both publicly declaring that the other individual was a man of honor.

We find an interesting example of this back-and-forth "negotiating" in Genesis 23. Abraham needed a place to inter Sarah, who had died in Hebron, but despite God's repeated promise the patriarch owned no land. So he approached the local people at the city gate (Gen. 23:10). "I am a resident alien among you; sell me a burial site" (verse 4, Tanakh).

The locals replied, "You are the elect of God among us. Bury your dead in the choicest of our burial places; none of us will withhold his burial place from you" (verse 6, Tanakh).

Abraham prostrated himself before the Hittite men and asked them to be his broker with an individual named Ephron (verse 8). "Let him sell me the cave of Machpelah that he owns. . . . Let him sell it to me, at the full price" (verse 9, Tanakh). It would not have been honorable for Abraham to have immediately confronted Ephron with his request. That would have been a negative challenge that would have required rebuff.

Ephron publicly responded, "No, my lord, hear me: I give you the field and I give you the cave that is in it" (verse 11, Tanakh). In this game of challenge and riposte, Ephron really had no intention of giving away valuable property—especially to Abraham, a wealthy foreigner. But both he and Abraham were behaving in such a way that each would retain his honor at the end of the negotiations. It would end up being a win-win situation for both.

Abraham bowed low once again, showing deference to Ephron and the other Hittites at the city gate (city gates were where people conducted business and other transactions). "Let me pay the price of the land; accept it from me, that I may bury my dead there" (verse 13, Tanakh).

Ephron: "My lord, do hear me! A piece of land worth four hundred shekels of silver—what is that between you and me? Go and bury your dead" (verse 15, Tanakh). Four times the expression "My lord, do hear me" or its equivalent appears in the story—twice by Abraham and twice by Ephron. It sounds strange to our ears, but neither man wanted to gain shame as a result of the negotiations. So each was playing the game of challenge and riposte with consummate skill. Notice that at this point in the haggling, Ephron indicates the price of the land—even though he is overtly saying that he would *give* the acreage to Abraham. Abraham now knew what the asking price was. (Some scholars consider it an exorbitant sum of money.)

"Abraham accepted Ephron's terms. Abraham paid out to Ephron . . . four hundred shekels of silver at the going merchants' rate. So Ephron's land in Machpelah, near Mamre—the field with its cave and all the trees anywhere within the confines of that field—passed to Abraham as his possession, in the presence of the Hittites, of all who entered the gate of his town. And then Abraham buried his wife Sarah in the cave. . . . Thus the field with its cave passed from the Hittites to Abraham, as a burial site" (verses 16-20, Tanakh).

And both Ephron and Abraham, having exhibited extreme courtesy, left with their bank account of honor intact, although Abraham's bank account of money had considerably diminished!

The same sort of thing should have taken place in Genesis 13 between Lot and Abraham (then Abram) when their servants began quarreling among one another. But Lot was not the sort of person who respected the niceties of society.

Abram started what should have been a series of negotiations by saying, "Is not the whole land before you? Let us separate: if you go north, I will go south; and if you to south, I will go north" (Gen. 13:9, Tanakh).

Lot should have responded, "Oh, no, Uncle Abram. Far be it from me to choose. Hear me out. *You* choose first." Abraham would have repeated his offer, and Lot should have again reacted as society expected an inferior to behave; but that's not how it went. The nephew didn't behave even as Abram's peer should have acted—as Ephron later did.

No. Instead, "Lot looked about him and saw how well watered was the whole plain of the Jordan, all of it . . . like the garden of the Lord" (verse 10, Tanakh). No haggling. No deference here. "So Lot chose for himself the whole plain of the Jordan, and Lot journeyed eastward" (verse 11, Tanakh). The nephew selected the best-looking land for himself, leaving the arid hill country and desert lands to his uncle. That's not how a respectful man would have behaved. But Lot was not that kind of person. His name probably meant "wrapped," and Lot was all wrapped up in himself.

When we read the Gospels, we notice that pretty much every time Jesus went public, someone else challenged Him. It meant that anyone who did so thereby conceded that Jesus was a worthy man—an honorable person. And when Jesus reacted with a riposte, He was showing that the person confronting Him was also honorable. "The fact that Jesus was so regularly challenged indicates . . . that he was a very honorable person who was worthy of allegiance and loyalty. It is to his credit that he was both envied (Matt. 27:18) and challenged" (Rohrbaugh, p. 21).

A challenge could be either positive or negative. Positive challenges included paying compliments, giving a present, asking for a favor, or volunteering to do something for the other person. If a man accepted such positive challenges, ancient culture expected that in order to maintain his own bank account of honor, he would have to respond similarly—maybe in kind. Thus one did not accept an invitation to a banquet without first deciding if the invitation came from a peer and if he, the invitee, was ready to return the favor later on. (Notice how Jesus went against His culture when He told His disciples to do something without expecting others to reciprocate.) Negative challenges were more hostile and confrontational in nature and included insulting the other party, threatening the other person physically, or slandering the other individual.

Jesus was the recipient of both positive and negative challenges during His public ministry. It was a positive challenge of sorts when an unnamed man offered to become one of Jesus' disciples (Matt. 8:19). But it was a negative challenge when certain spies asked Jesus if it was lawful to pay tribute to Caesar (Luke 20:22).

At one point in Jesus' short career, His own family came to get Him because His behavior was causing them to lose honor and gain shame (Mark 3:21—the KJV says they were His "friends," but the Greek word here refers to His kinfolk, who came to arrest or capture Him because people had begun to consider Him to be crazy; compare verse 31). If His family members were of the artisan class, as were Joseph and Jesus, they already had a low bank account of honor and could hardly afford to lose even a modicum of it.

We've covered a lot of ground in this chapter, but now when you read your Bible you can be sensitive to issues of shame and honor. As a result you'll be able to better understand why certain biblical male characters behaved the way they did and why they said some of the things they said. It's difficult to underestimate the importance of the role that concepts of honor and shame played in daily life throughout the ancient Near East—the world of the Bible writers . . . and readers.

CHAPTER 5

Cultural Norms— Patriarchal Society

Most of us Western readers "know" that the ancient Near East was a patriarchal society, but we aren't always sure what that entails. The word "patriarchal" comes from two Greek roots: patria, which means father, and archï, which means rulership. In oversimplified terms, in a patriarchal society the males have the (most) power and so count for more than females. In fact, in such societies one rarely hears female voices at all.

The point is that in such cultures the men have more clout, authority, and voice than do the women. It's not that the women have no social power, for they generally do have some. However, in a patriarchal society the power is disproportionately in the hands of men, usually older males. Power and ownership get traced through the male line back through one generation into another. Men formed the society and its rules and so benefited the most from its mores.

But what exactly does a patriarchal society "look" like? There's no single description that can fit all patriarchal societies, because the amount of power that men have versus the number of rights that women have varies from culture to culture. Not all patriarchal societies equally oppress women, even though in all patriarchal societies men exert the most power and have the most honor. But we can hazard a few examples that will illustrate what a patriarchal society can look like.

A Modern Semi-patriarchal Society

First of all, we need only to take a look around us. Although our society today is not radically patriarchal, it still shows preference for men over women in many ways. Have you noticed enthusiastic acceptance of what is commonly called "feminism"? I doubt it. What about "women's rights"? Do you know how long it has been that American women have had the legal right to vote? They gained it in 1920. Not that long ago, huh?

When a woman gets married, typically she loses her "maiden name" and takes the surname of her husband. (In recent years a growing number of women opt for a hyphenated last name: Mary Smith-Jones. A very few married women in America continue to go by their "maiden name.") And the children born to these marriages carry whose last name for their identity? The mother's—the woman who endured gut-wrenching bouts of morning sickness, toted that burgeoning weight of the fetus around in her body for nine months, and suffered the agony of childbirth? No! Instead, the newborn receives its surname from the father.

In American society, who holds the majority of positions of power—men or women? Has there yet been a female president of the United States? a female vice president? How many female generals are there in the Army compared to the number of male generals? In American businesses, are men and women equally represented as CEOs? According to Martha Burk, head of the National Council of Women's Organizations, in corporate America women constitute only 13.6 percent of board members (http://www.cluw.org/programs-payequity.html).

In the job market, who earns more on average—a man or a woman? In 2002 women earned $30,724, while men earned $40,668 (*ibid.*). Did you know that worldwide men earn 90 percent of the income and own 99 percent of the property? According to the 2000 census, American women made $0.73 to every $1 made by men. This means that on average women earn $27 less than men for every $100 worth of work done.

The shocking part is that these figures represent what is happening in American culture—a presumably progressive society. The plight of women in patriarchal cultures around the world even today is much worse. We've all heard horror stories about what happens to women in Afghanistan or Africa or . . . The fact is that the status of women in the biblical world is closer to the plight of women in these traditional societies than to the rights of women in contemporary America. But more about that a bit later.

A few years ago my church's Bible study lesson series dealt with Ephesians 5:22-24 and 6:1-9. As I sat in class hearing the discussion, I found it rather interesting. Twenty people were in the class, 11 of them women. However, most of the discussion about what Paul meant when he instructed that women should be in subjection to their husbands came from the men.

The husbands in the class acknowledged that their wives should be in subjection to them, though no one actually came out and said, "I'm the boss." But having exerted their authority over women, the men also suggested that husbands should generously and often "let their wives have their own way," because there was really nothing meritorious in men always dominating everything. Theoretically, the man can do so because he's head of the wife, who must remain in submission to him, but as a considerate Christian he won't be selfish and always insist on doing things his way. Yet this in a sense flies in the face of Paul's clear command that wives should be subjugated to their husbands in *everything* (Eph. 5:24).

My pastor, who was sitting next to me, tried to goad me into adding my own "heretical" comments by pointing out that some biblical interpreters insist that this passage is "culturally conditioned."

He referred to the outline of Paul's discussion, which fell into three parts: (1) relationships between spouses, which is further subdivided into (a) wives should be in subjection to their husbands and (b) husbands should love their wives (though wives are not commanded—and hence not obligated—to love their husbands); (2) relationships between parents and children, which is further subdivided into (a) children should obey their parents (the words "in the Lord" are not in many manuscripts) and (b) fathers shouldn't make their children angry; and (3) relationships between masters and slaves, which is subdivided into (a) slaves should obey their masters and (b) masters shouldn't threaten their slaves.

"Now, which of these three sections is culturally conditioned?" the pastor asked. "We would all agree with the second section that commands children to obey their parents. So that's not culturally conditioned. What, then, about the part dealing with slavery? Is that culturally conditioned, or isn't it? And what about the first part that tells wives to be subject to their husbands? If the second section is not culturally conditioned, why would we think that the first part is?"

I held my peace, but as I understand matters, all Scripture is culturally conditioned, and every reading of it is also culturally conditioned. We can no more get away from cultural conditioning than we can escape from our human nature. Every communication given is culturally conditioned, and every recipient of a communication is culturally conditioned in his or her reading of it. Cultural conditioning is not inherently evil. It's there, just as the air we breathe is there. This book that I've written is culturally conditioned, and your understanding of what you read in these pages will also be culturally conditioned.

In my estimation the passage in Ephesians 5 and 6 is a good example of something written in a patriarchal society, even though Paul seems to be trying to tone down patriarchy somewhat. He was writing within a patriarchal society to people who were conditioned by that patriarchal culture and urging that the subjection go both ways: "Submit to one another out of reverence for Christ" (Eph. 5:21, NIV). In this context of a patriarchal society, we see how God through His servant Paul can work within that culture, suggesting ways that would lead to mutual subjugation.

At first reading, Paul's counsel in this passage seems strange to us, and probably it should. Today we read these verses from our Western perspective, and the Ephesians saw them from within their patriarchal culture. Paul's perspective was still within the framework of a patriarchy, but he also was setting a trajectory that led away from it—at least in its most obvious forms. That's why he could also write that "there is neither Jew nor Greek, there is neither bond nor free, there is neither male nor female: for ye are all one in Christ Jesus" (Gal. 3:28).

Women in the Ancient Near East

Generally speaking, the ancient Near East regarded women as mentally, physically, emotionally, and spiritually inferior to men. In some instances society viewed them as even a distinct species from men!

The head of the family in ancient Rome was called *pater familias*. It could be any male who was not subordinate to another *pater familias*. He owned all property—land, houses, furnishings, and people within the household. If he so wished, he could resort to capital punishment for any person under his authority. It was not unheard-of for a father to sell his children into slavery or give away a son to a childless friend. Mothers had no legal rights and were expected to stay at home while they tended the children and did all the housekeeping if the family was not rich. However, unlike women in other ancient patriarchal societies, she could call upon friends and frequent public places such as the forums, the baths, the public libraries, the temples, and the amphitheater. Roman women could never hold any public office. A girl was ready for marriage when she turned 14.

Roman wives tended to have more freedoms than did Greek wives, although the two ancient cultures had many similarities. In ancient Greece the women were not citizens and basically had no legal status. Women had to stay pretty much in comparative seclusion, living in separate rooms from the men. If they ventured outside the house, they needed supervision. Athenian women, for example, were under the watch of a *kyrios* (male lord or guardian). The *kyrios* was her father if she was young, her husband if she was married, or whoever was her closest male birth relative if she was single. Women could own personal property such as clothing, jewelry, or slaves, but they could not purchase anything other than cheap items and could not own real estate or enter into any contract.

The idea of marrying because of romantic love was not a concern then, unlike today. The chief reasons for marriage were control of property and the expansion of the family. Adult males arranged the marriages and viewed them pretty much a business transaction. Upon marriage the ownership of the woman passed from the father to the husband. If an Athenian man caught someone having sex with his wife, daughter, or any other female relative, he could legally kill that man on the spot. Sexual intercourse for pleasure was not something a Greek man had with his wife. For that he had recourse to prostitutes, concubines, and younger men. (Many Greek—and Roman—men were what we today would call bisexual. Even macho army generals had young lads for lovers. Some Greeks, for instance, regarded having sex with a woman as "unnatural," whereas having sex with a young male was seen as very "natural." Nero, infamous emperor of Rome, took both women and men as spouses.)

The extent of the subjugation of women varied throughout ancient Mesopotamia, depending on the time and the national culture. Some societies granted women more status than did others—although all were patriarchal societies.

Babylon, especially as demonstrated by Hammurabi's law code (c.

1780 B.C.), considered sons and daughters the private property of the father, but the wife had many rights. Illicit sexual activity with another man's wife was punished just as other forms of stealing were. Society, however, allowed men more sexual liberties than it did women. Men generally owned property, although there appears to have been no legal sanction against women possessing real estate as well. Marriages were typically arranged by the families of those involved, although it may be that both the woman and the man had some input into the decision. People simply did not write much about this aspect of marriage.

If a husband suspected his wife of having an adulterous affair, the two of them could appear before a priest, and the wife could solemnly testify under oath of her innocence. Then her husband could accept her back. However, if another individual accused a man's wife of adultery, she had to swear under oath to her innocence and then undergo an "ordeal" to prove her guilt or innocence. The ordeal consisted of jumping into the river. Since few women knew how to swim in ancient Babylon, most women drowned and were therefore presumed guilty.

According to Hammurabi's Code, a man had to divide his estate among his sons after he had given an adequate dowry for each daughter and a suitable bride price for each son. If he was unable to do so because of an untimely death, his heirs were legally bound to provide the proper financial arrangements prior to dividing the remaining assets. Should a man have had multiple wives who had given birth to children, then each son received an equal share in the estate. As for a woman who had given birth to children by two husbands, upon her death her dowry was to be divided equally among her sons by both marriages.

Although ancient Egypt was also a patriarchal society, women there tended to fare much better than elsewhere in the ancient Near East. They enjoyed nearly as many rights as did the men. Although ancient Egypt had legal distinctions, they were based more on social class than on gender. Women could own real estate, sell and buy goods, and even institute divorce proceedings. Nor did they need a man to instigate legal proceedings, but could initiate litigation on their own. A woman could even remain single and live without being under the control of a male. Real estate passed from one generation to the next through the mother's side of the family. Although male priests were generally in charge of temple affairs, many female priests also existed. Some women even ended up being a pharaoh.

Egyptian women could freely appear in public. They could work outside the house and did not have to wear a veil when they ventured into the public arena. Marriage was less complicated than elsewhere in the ancient world. Girls as young as 8 could get married, although most were probably around 12 or 14. Egypt had no formal marriage ceremonies, and the couple did not exchange rings. The woman simply left her home to live with her husband, who might have more than one wife if he was wealthy. Men could have adulterous relationships without sanctions (though some might be forced into a divorce), but women who committed adultery were subject to capital punishment. Giving birth was especially important, even though ancient Egypt used the first known contraceptive—crocodile dung!

Egypt had a significant group of female physicians. Lady Peseshet was the first known example. At one point Egypt had at least 100 female doctors serving their country.

Women in Ancient Israel

Israelite society in both the Old and New Testaments was highly patriarchal and patrilineal, and evidence for this comes from both Scripture and nonbiblical sources. The Hebrew expression, for instance, that we could translate as "family" is *bêt 'Çb*, which means literally "house of the father." Property passed down through the male line, and "women [were] to some extent either aliens or transients within their family of residence. Married women [were] outsiders in the household of their husband and sons, while daughters [were] prepared from birth to leave their father's household and transfer loyalty to a husband's house and lineage" (*Anchor Bible Dictionary*, Vol. VI, p. 952). The life of a female in ancient Hebrew society would hardly be something that modern American women would pine for!

Biblical culture considered women as dangerous—easily falling into sexual dalliances that would detract from the family's honor and a ready source for ritual uncleanness. It was the men who offered the sacrifices in the cult center (the tabernacle/sanctuary and later the Temple), and it was the priests (always male) who carried out the religious rituals.

The rightful domain for women was in the house and at the town well. The proper domain for men was outside the home—in the fields and at the city gate, where society meted out justice. Women did not typically eat with the men. They prepared the food, then retired to a secluded spot while the men devoured the meal (see Gen. 18:9).

Society deemed it scandalous for women to keep company with men, because such behavior could ensnare the men into sexual dalliances and/or cause the men to become unclean if the woman was menstruating. It must have been truly outrageously shameful in the eyes of proper society that a group of women accompanied Jesus in His ministry. People would have regarded them as shameless, when they should have been shame-ful.

Leviticus 27:1-6 gives a sliding scale for the worth of people involved in making a vow. The text doesn't tell us much about the purpose of the vow, but it does list a monetary value for people as follows:

infant males (from 1 month to 5 years)	= 5 shekels
infant females (from 1 month to 5 years)	= 3 shekels
minor males (from 5 years to 20 years)	= 20 shekels
minor females (from 5 years to 20 years)	= 10 shekels
adult males (from 20 years to 60 years)	= 50 shekels
adult females (from 20 years to 60 years)	= 30 shekels
elderly males (from 60 years up)	= 15 shekels
elderly females (from 60 years up)	= 10 shekels

Scholars have proposed various explanations for the different monetary amounts, but have not reached any consensus. For our purposes in this chapter, we need only notice that in each instance the passage ranks females as of lesser monetary value than males. This variation really shouldn't surprise us, because it was a patriarchal society—although some commentators point out that the amounts for women do indicate that society considered them to have high value, just not as high as men.

The Decalogue, said to come directly from God Himself, lists the wife with slave, ox, ass, and "any thing" owned by the man. "Thou shalt not covet thy neighbour's house, thou shalt not covet thy neighbour's wife, nor his manservant, nor his maidservant, nor his ox, nor his ass, nor any thing that is thy neighbour's" (Ex. 20:17). With that concept in mind one can recognize a certain logic behind the way it bans adultery (verse 14). A

kind of stealing (forbidden in verse 15), adultery involved the taking of another man's possession. A woman was subject to her father until transferred
by marriage to her husband.

Families arranged marriages, and they usually did not function in a romantic way but rather served as an economic relationship. The girl was
usually 12 or 13 when she married. Early on, the man's family paid a bride
price (Hebrew *mohar*), because this served as a form of financial restitution
to the bride's family as well as a kind of social glue that cemented relationships between the two families. In later centuries the bride price was purely
a symbolic token.

We often talk about the biblical blueprint for marriage and family and
assume that the biblical world had only one type of family—something
akin to our nuclear family—that received sanction in Scripture. However,
it would be more correct to talk about the biblical *patterns* of family found
throughout Scripture. In fact, we see at least eight different family config-
urations or types in the Bible. They are as follows.

1. Nuclear family—Genesis 2:24 talks about a man leaving his family
of origin, joining with a woman, consummating the marriage, and living
as a new family group. We do find differences between the customs and
laws of contemporary North Americans and those of the ancient Israelites.
A woman presented by her father as a virgin but who could not provide
evidence that she had been one could be stoned to death by the men of
her village (Deut. 22:13-21). There appears to have been no similar penalty
for men who engaged in consensual premarital sexual activity.

2. Polygynist marriage—When finances allowed, a man would marry
as many women as he wished. The more wives a man had, the higher his
social standing. For kings, many of their wives came from the royal families of other countries, so marrying them was a way of ensuring peace
between nations. The new wives would join the man and his other wives
in an already established household.

We find numerous examples of polygyny in Scripture. Lamech was the
first recorded polygamist with two wives—Adah and Zillah (Gen. 4:19).
Esau acquired three wives—Judith, Bashemath, and Mahalath (Gen. 26:34;
28:9). Ashur married two women—Helah and Naarah (1 Chron. 4:5).
Elkanah had two wives—Peninnah and Hannah (1 Sam. 1:4, 8);
Shaharaim, two wives—Hushim and Baara (1 Chron. 8:8); and Abijah, 14

wives (2 Chron. 13:21). Jehoiada married two women (2 Chron. 24:3). We won't multiply examples.

3. A man with one or more wives and some concubines—This was a variation on polygamous marriage. In addition to his numerous wives, a man could also keep numerous concubines. Such women held an even lower status than did the wives, though it was a legal relationship. As implied in Genesis 21:10, a man could dismiss his concubine when he no longer wanted her.

Once again we find in the Bible numerous examples of this type of marriage arrangement. Jacob had two wives—Leah and Rachel—and two concubines. Gideon had at least one concubine. Caleb had two. King David had many wives, including Michal, Ahinoam, Abigail, Eglah, Bathsheba, as well as the 10 women who had been Saul's wives—whom God gave to David when he replaced Saul as king (2 Sam. 12:8). Solomon had 700 wives from royalty plus 300 concubines. Rehoboam had 18 wives and 60 concubines.

4. Levirate marriage—The name of this type of marriage derives from the Latin word *levir*, which means "brother-in-law." It calls for a brother-in-law to take as wife a woman widowed without having given birth to a son. Biblical society considered their firstborn son to be sired by the deceased husband. Scripture had God Himself commanding levirate marriage (Deut. 25:5-10).

5. A man, a woman, and her property, a female slave—Abraham had Sarah as a wife; then he took the slave girl Hagar as a concubine. Upon Sarah's death he married Keturah. In addition, he also had other multiple but unnamed concubines (Gen. 25:1, 6). This type of marriage had some points of similarity to polygamous marriage. However, Hagar's status as a human slave in a plural marriage with two free individuals makes it sufficiently different to warrant separate treatment.

6. A male soldier and female prisoners of war—Numbers 31:1-18 describes how the Israelite army killed every adult Midianite male in battle. Moses then ordered the slaughter of most of the captives, including all of the male children. Only the lives of 32,000 women—all virgins—were spared. Some of the latter were given to YHWH, but the Israelite soldiers took most as captives of war. Deuteronomy 21:11-14 describes how each captive woman would shave her head, pare her nails, and be left alone to mourn the loss of her families, friends, and freedom. After a month passed, the captive virgins would be required to marry their soldier conquerors.

7. *A male rapist and his victim*—A female virgin who was not engaged to be married and who had been raped had to marry her attacker, no matter what her feelings were toward the rapist. A man could become married by simply sexually attacking a woman that appealed to him then paying his new father-in-law 50 shekels of silver (Ex. 22:16; Deut. 22:28, 29).

8. *A male and female slave*—A slave owner could assign one of his female slaves to one of his male slaves as a wife. We have no indication that anyone consulted the slave women involved prior to such a transaction. During the period of the Hebrew Scriptures Israelite women sold into slavery by their fathers remained slaves forever. When a male slave left his owner, the marriage would normally be terminated, and his wife would stay behind with any children that she may have given birth to. But he could elect to remain a slave if he wished (Ex. 21:4-6).

Today we find such practices appalling, but apparently these various marriage/family conventions did not bother God—at least not enough for Him to ban them.

In certain instances He enacted laws that regulated some of the practices. For instance, God regulated polygamy. He said that multiple marriages were OK as long as the husband didn't shortchange his first wife in food and clothing (Ex. 21:10). As late as the New Testament the church allowed polygamy for Christians—but not for its elders and deacons (1 Tim. 3:2, 12).

In other cases God specifically commanded a practice. He decreed that a rape victim marry her attacker (Ex. 22:16; Deut. 22:28, 29), that a marriage of slaves be dissolved when the male slave gained his freedom (Ex. 21:4-6), and that levirate marriage was acceptable (Deut. 25:5-10).

In one case God took responsibility for a specific practice. He told David that among the blessings that He had given him as new king were the wives of Saul, the previous king (2 Sam. 12:8). And in other instances the Lord simply ignored the custom. For example, He remained silent about concubinage.

God could have condemned such practices, as He did other forms of behavior in His law code. But He chose to ignore these various permutations on marriage and family that today we find repugnant. Yet He tells us that He found other practices abhorrent, ones that many today engage in without a second thought. For instance, He opposed eating pork, but allowed a rape victim to marry her rapist. God found the wearing of blended cloth (what is your dress or your trousers made from—a blended fabric?) more offensive than forced marriages of virgins taken as prisoners of war. And He had more to say about plowing with a yoked ox and donkey (if you visited an agricultural society as a missionary and found people doing this, would you think that God was upset with this practice and so try to correct it?) than having multiple wives plus numerous concubines.

It appears that God can adapt to various cultures—including a patriarchal society. Additionally, He can accept various marriage practices without uttering a complaint—not even a single word of condemnation. Most of this should not surprise us, though, when we realize that Israelite society—along with all the other cultures in the ancient Near East—was a patriarchal one. But it is truly quite different from the ideals that we hold in Western society today.

The ancient Near East considered children—especially sons—as a gift from God. Should a woman have no children, society generally regarded it as her fault. She was supposed to be the field into which her husband planted his seed. If she didn't produce children, she was not a fertile field— and maybe was even a resistant field!

Ancient culture often viewed women as birthing machines, which may be understandable in light of the child mortality rate at that time. Society needed many children because the death rate was terribly high back then. The estimated mortality rates for the first century suggest that more than 30 percent of babies died at birth—as did many mothers. (Because many women died during childbirth, many men ended up with multiple wives, though not necessarily all at the same time.) Thirty-three percent of children who reached their first birthday perished before they turned 6 years old. Of those who remained after they had celebrated their sixth birthday, almost 60 percent died before they reached 16. Seventy-five percent of the survivors were dead before their twenty-sixth birthday. Only about 3 percent reached age 60. This means that when Jesus was crucified, He was probably older than 80 percent of those who clamored for His death.

Crop fertility was also a primary concern for local farmers. They needed abundant harvests because the ratio of seed planted to crop reaped was a fraction of what it is today. In addition, most of what they harvested they then had to turn over to the absentee landlord, and much of the seed left would go for the next planting.

During the first century, for example, a few peasants owned their own small plots (anywhere from 6 to 16.8 acres), whereas many—tenants—worked the land for wealthy absentee landlords. Typically these farmers were one drought or crop failure away from financial disaster and perhaps starvation. Farming techniques didn't bring bumper crops such as we know today. Instead of our yields of 40 times what is sown, back then one was fortunate if the crop was 10 to 15 times the amount of seed sown. Most peasants and tenants could keep for their own personal use as much as one fifth or as little as one thirteenth of the crop.

By the way, those statistics help explain why those in the ancient Near East had such an obsession about fertility. Many of the gods that people worshipped were thought to have been responsible for fertility. Archaeologists have found even in Israelite settlements scads of figurines of naked women with pronounced erogenous zones. They appear to have been fertility goddesses cherished by Hebrew women who were supposed to have been monotheists! Many of the indigenous religions were fertility ones in which male worshippers would have sexual intercourse with sacred temple prostitutes.

Such "worship" sounds rather vulgar to us, but it and other similar practices had a certain rationale behind it. For the people in the ancient Near East, it was a logical way of worship. Anthropologists and sociologists call this an example of "sympathetic magic" employing the "law of similarity." The idea behind sympathetic magic is quite simple. Sympathetic magic is based on the metaphysical belief that like affects like or that "likes produce likes." The idea is that someone can produce the desired effect by imitating it. If the wanted effect is fertility—many children and abundant harvests—then one engages in acts of fertility. The cause-and-effect relationship is that the effect resembles its cause.

More Hebrew Sexual Inequities

Although a woman in marriage could retain her own real estate (if she had any), when the family went bankrupt, both the husband and the wife faced the consequences, such as being sold into slavery. Although it was not common, a woman could inherit property from her father or husband (Num. 26:33; 27:1-11). However, most real estate among the Hebrew people was transferred from one generation to the next through the males, not the females.

A husband could obtain divorce papers—a "writ of divorce"—quite readily, but a wife had no recourse to divorce. Society typically frowned upon a divorced woman, and she had a difficult existence—unless she was able to return to her original family. Mosaic law defined adultery as chiefly something that the woman, not the man, did.

Now when you read Scripture, you can be more sensitive to those cultural norms that marked the patriarchal society that every biblical person lived in, which they took for granted as the "normal" way of life— just as we assume that our way of life is the "normal" one. And when you read about women in the Bible, you can now be more sensitive to how they act (if they appear at all in a story) and be more aware of what they say (if they engage in any dialogue in the narrative).

CHAPTER 6

Cultural Norms— Patronage and Clientage

Most people in Palestine during the first century were living on the edge when it came to material goods. They were just eking out a living. Here's what we think we know about life for the common person during Jesus' lifetime.

As mentioned in the previous chapter, many babies died at birth—as did many mothers. Children also perished at alarming rates. A large number of teenagers had already lost their fathers and mothers. By the time most people reached adulthood they suffered from all manner of diseases.

It isn't easy to come up with precise figures, that everyone can agree upon, of the economic situation in first-century Palestine. In fact, various contemporary scholars differ on these points. However, we can regard these statistics as ballpark figures.

Back then there was no middle class as we know it. The elites stood at the top of society, dominating the nonelites, the peasants, and those even less fortunate. The elites and their retainers comprised the ruling classes, and they included political as well as religious leaders. The elites constituted somewhere between 1 and 10 percent of the population, but enjoyed two-thirds of the wealth and owned some 50 percent of the land. Herod the Great, for instance, claimed 25 to 33 percent of the grain grown in his domain and 50 percent of the fruit harvested. The priests probably owned 15 percent of the land.

So the nonelites—the peasants, and below them the artisans (about 5 percent), and beneath them others such as slaves, prostitutes, beggars, bandits, and the homeless—made up the rest of the population but had at most only one third of the wealth, including land. The poor, which included most of the nonelites, were generally regarded with disdain by the elites. At least 90 to 97 percent of the people were illiterate.

The peasants consisted mostly of farmers. Some owned their own small plots (anywhere from six to 17 acres), whereas many—tenants—worked the land for wealthy absentee landlords. Researchers estimate that a grown person needed at least 1.5 acres of planted farmland and the same acreage of unplanted land (for pasturing animals) to provide a subsistence level. Many peasants owned just six acres of land to support an extended family.

Most of the crops consisted of wheat, barley, millet, rice, onions, garlic, leeks, squashes, cabbages, radishes, beets, olives, grapes, figs, dates, lentils, and beans. Typically such farmers were one drought or crop failure away from financial disaster and perhaps starvation. Farming techniques didn't bring bumper crops such as we know today.

Many peasants had already lost their small plots of land because they couldn't pay their debts. "By late in the first century nearly half the arable land in the entire region of Galilee had been accumulated . . . by just three families. In fact, the entire population of a whole village (Bene Hassan) had become indebted tenants of one of these absentee landlords" (Rohrbaugh, p. 6). The Roman government took between 35 to 40 percent of a peasant's livelihood (Bruce J. Malina and Richard L. Rohrbaugh, *Social-Science Commentary on the Synoptic Gospels*, p. 376). Additionally, the Jewish people had to pay religious levies—tithe, soil tax, head tax, cost of lambs for sacrifice, and the cost of vows made.

Many tenant farmers were deeply in debt—usually to the absentee landlord to whom they owed rent in addition to their repayment of the loan. Frequently they had to pay high interest rates for the loans, which drove many into abject destitution or even imprisonment. Some former tenant farmers became either beggars, who looked for alms, or bandits, who robbed the rich whenever they had the opportunity.

Douglas E. Oatman has suggested that the expression "forgive us our debts. . . . And lead us not into temptation, but deliver us from evil [the evil one]" (Matt. 6:12, 13) in the Lord's Prayer is the peasant's request that he not be hauled into court because of his unpaid debts—especially if he had to appear before a crooked judge—"the evil one."

It shouldn't surprise us, then, that although Jesus belonged to the artisan class, which society generally considered as below the peasant class, He told a lot of stories about farming and indebtedness. After all, they were topics that His audiences knew firsthand.

Patronage and Clientage

It was in this socioeconomic context that the practice of *clientela*—patronage and clientage—was terribly important. Patrons were well-to-do individuals who gave money (or other benefactions or aid) to cities and to individual persons who were below them socially. Ancient documentary evidence attests to the widespread practice.

Specific terminology referred to the three aspects of this popular relationship. The socially superior individual was called in Latin and Greek the *patronus, patrona, euergetes,* and *prostatis.* The beneficence was known as *beneficium, meritum, favor, gratia* (grace), *charis* (grace; favor). And the client was called *cliens* or *salutatores.* The relationship between the two persons—the superior and the inferior—went by the term *fides* (faithfulness). Sometimes an intermediary—a broker—served to get the two individuals together.

The benefaction or help for individuals could involve monetary aid, provision of food, personal protection, job advancement, manumission (the freeing of slaves), an adjustment in taxation, help with legal issues, employment, and other valuable gifts. The benefaction for cities might be the erection of a statue, the construction of a temple or theater, sponsorship of a public event, underwriting the cost of paving a street, or something else that would enhance the status of the city itself.

The ratio of those needing aid to the wealthy elites was enormous, and even the most wealthy family would find it impossible to help everyone in need. So benefactors selected "worthy" people to assist, even though people were not supposed to provide patronage from selfish reasons. They were to give for the sheer love of giving. Seneca the Younger, Roman philosopher, orator, and playwright who lived from c. 3 B.C. to A.D. 65, wrote: "He who gives benefits imitates the gods, he who seeks a return, money-lenders" (*De beneficiis* 3. 15. 4). Patrons did have the right to consider the potential for gratitude that the client might have, but not the prospective beneficiary's ability to repay the favor.

Although clients were not expected to reciprocate with any material benefits, they were supposed to offer public gratitude, thereby making deposits to the patron's honor bank. Clients in Rome, for instance, would show up early in the morning at the patron's house and announce publicly how generous the patron was and how impossible it was for them to repay such beneficence. Also clients would run errands for their patrons, gather information through the gossip channels, attend funerals for the patrons' family members, or even testify in court on behalf of the benefactors. The ultimate show of honor on the part of the client was to remember the patron in one's last will and testament. If clients did not respond by showering patrons with honor, they brought shame upon themselves, and society viewed them as being terrible criminals, even though no law actually legislated against ungrateful clients. Just as patrons provided benefactions freely, so clients provided honor freely in return.

The relationship established between patron and client typically was to last forever—an ongoing relationship. The patron might call the client "friend." People often used the word "faith" to describe the relationship—but in the sense of dependability. Both the patron and the client depended upon each other to maintain a mutual relationship of trust. The client trusted the patron's generosity, and the patron assumed that the client would respond with public gratitude. The patron would not mention the gift once the benefaction had been received, but the client would always speak about it—to anyone who would listen.

The New Testament depicts God as the patron, lost souls saved as His clients, and Jesus Himself as the broker—the go-between who linked needy humanity to divine beneficence. It's also important to remember that God, the patron, took the initiative to reach out to sinful human beings through Jesus Christ, the broker. The dynamic of divine patronage and human clientage established the relationship that we commonly call "salvation."

We see an example of patronage and clientage when Jesus healed the 10 men with leprosy as told in Luke 17. Ten lepers encountered Jesus as He entered a village, the name of which we don't know. They called out, "Jesus, Master, have mercy on us" (verse 13).

Jesus told them to go to the priests to be inspected. As the 10 lepers headed toward the Temple they discovered that "they were cleansed" (verse 14). The point in reporting to the priests, of course, was so that the religious authorities would declare them clean and they could then offer the requisite sacrificial ritual and once more join normal society.

At this point Jesus had become the patron, and the 10 men had become His clients. Jesus, the great benefactor, had provided healing—a wonderful gift. It was now their responsibility as clients to provide Him with honor.

Immediately one of the healed men "turned back, and with a loud voice glorified God, and fell down on his face at his feet, giving [Jesus] thanks" (verses 15, 16). It was the proper behavior for a client, but only one of the 10 acted as a client should. "And he was a Samaritan" (verse 16). Only one of the 10—a Samaritan at that—acknowledged his new status as client.

Jesus Himself wondered what had happened to the other men. Where were *they*? "Were there not ten cleansed? but where are the nine? There are not found that returned to give glory to God, save this stranger" (verses 17, 18). Jesus then turned to the healed Samaritan and said, "Arise, go thy way: thy faith hath made thee whole" (verse 19).

In Luke 8 we find another interesting story. Jesus and His disciples had hopped into a boat and sailed to the country of the Gadarenes. When they disembarked at their destination, a raving demoniac who lived among the tombs met them. Naked, he screamed like a maniac. Even chains could not keep him under control, because with supernatural strength he would burst his fetters. When he saw Jesus, he fell down and pleaded with Jesus not to torment him—as if Christ were in the habit of tormenting people!

With a few calm words Jesus exorcised the demons, and the man became quiet and tame while the demons entered a herd of pigs that promptly stampeded off a cliff and into the lake. Certain onlookers became fearful themselves and rushed into the nearby town, shouting out what had happened.

Jesus was the benefactor here. The demoniac was His client. And Jesus gave the man a valuable gift—sanity, peace of mind.

"Now the man out of whom the devils were departed besought him that he might be with" Jesus (Luke 8:38). The healed man wanted to accompany his Benefactor wherever Jesus went. It was surely an understandable response to so wonderful a gift.

"But Jesus sent him away, saying, Return to thine own house, and shew how great things God hath done unto thee. And he went his way, and published throughout the whole city how great things Jesus had done unto him" (verses 38, 39).

Just as a grateful client should, the man returned to the village and told everyone he met about Jesus, the great benefactor, and what He had done for him, a lowly client. It was exactly how one expected clients to behave. Jesus was a generous benefactor, and the restored man was a grateful client.

One of the ongoing arguments among Christians has been the relationship of faith and works. The internal squabbling about this important issue began in the early days of the apostolic church and has continued to this day. There even seems to have been a difference of perspective between the progressive apostle Paul and Jesus' own conservative brother James.

The issue, however, becomes resolved quite readily when one understands salvation as the benefaction that (1) God the patron offers (2) through Jesus the broker (3) to sinful humans, the clients. Through Jesus Christ, God holds out the most wonderful benefaction of all—the gift of salvation from sin and the gift of eternal life. It is hardly a reciprocal relationship between peers, because we are far inferior and subordinate to God and can hardly repay Him with anything that comes near the value of the salvation that He bestows so freely upon us. We didn't do anything to merit such benefaction, and we can't do anything to reimburse God for it. His gift to us is of incomparable value.

However, by accepting God's patronage, we become part of His clientage. A relationship of faith—dependability and reliability—has been established. God never counted the cost when He provided the benefaction of salvation. Nonetheless, it is expected of clients to respond with clearly manifested forms of gratitude. And so each morning, at the start of the day, we ask our divine Benefactor if there is anything we might do for Him that day—not that we're trying to reciprocate in kind, because we can't, but that from deep-felt appreciation we feel obligated to serve Him and sing His praises whenever and wherever we can.

Among the terms the ancients used in connection with patronage and clientage were the Latin word *gratia* and the Greek word *charis*. Both words mean the same thing, and in English we often translate them as "grace." We Christians use the word all the time: saved by grace—God's grace, of course, as mediated by Jesus. In the context of patronage and clientage the Latin and Greek words denoted three distinct but related aspects of *clientela*: grace (1) the attitude of the patron, (2) the benefaction itself, and (3) the attitude of the client toward the gift.

In fact, an ancient sculpture known as the *Three Graces* depicted three young goddesses. Dancing hand-in-hand in a circle, they symbolized the three aspects of *clientela*. Seneca unpacked the meaning inherent in this piece of art: "Why do the sisters hand in hand dance in a ring which returns upon itself? For the reason that a benefit passing in its course from hand to hand returns nevertheless to the giver; the beauty of the whole is destroyed if the course is anywhere broken, and it has most beauty if it is continuous and maintains an uninterrupted succession. . . . Their faces are cheerful, as are ordinarily the faces of those who bestow or receive benefits. They are young because the memory of benefits ought not to grow old. They are maidens because benefits are pure and holy and undefiled in the eyes of all; [their robes] are transparent because benefits desire to be seen" (*De beneficiis* 1. 3. 2-5).

As Sophocles, a Greek playwright who lived from c. 496 B.C.–406 B.C., put it: "Favor [*charis*] is always giving birth to favor [*charin*]" (*Ajax* 522). "Grace, then, held two parties together in a bond of reciprocal exchanges" (David A. deSilva, p. 118). That is why the squabble over law versus grace and works versus faith is basically futile. The terms are not really antonyms, though they may be paradoxical.

"We are presented with something of a paradox. Just as the favor was freely bestowed, so the response must be free and uncoerced. Nonetheless, that response is at the same time necessary and unavoidable for honorable persons. . . . Gratitude is never a formal obligation. There is no advance calculation of or agreed-on return for the gift given. Nevertheless the recipient of a favor knows that he or she stands under the necessity of returning favor when favor has been received" (*ibid.*, p. 113).

Suzerainty Treaties

In the Old Testament we read about a practice (in effect long before the practice of patronage in Greek and Rome) that had some similarities (as well as some significant dissimilarities) to the *clientela* of the first century—the "cutting" of a covenant. To understand the significance of such Old Testament covenants, we need to become aware of the general practice of covenant making in the ancient Near East.

When the king of one city-state conquered another city-state or wanted to cement relationships with another city-state, he would establish a suzerainty treaty (also known as a covenant) with that other king. The Hittite rulers, among others, were especially adept at preparing suzerainty treaties, and archaeologists have found and translated a number of them. "The large number of international treaties preserved in texts from all over the ANE [ancient Near Eastern] world is dramatic witness to the importance of covenants in ancient social and political life" (*Anchor Bible Dictionary*, Vol. I, p. 1180). Some of these ancient documents date to near the invention of writing for other than bookkeeping purposes.

Sometimes such treaties obligated both parties to certain behavior, and scholars refer to them as "parity treaties." Much of the time, however, covenants were one-sided, having been imposed by a superior upon his vassal, and so it was the subjugated king who had to comply with all the stipulations set forth within the document.

Although not all covenants slavishly adhered to the same pattern, in general the treaties made up a distinct genre of written documents. A typical covenant might contain the following elements:

identification of the covenant maker; the covenant that Suppiluliumas enacted with Aziras, king of Amurru, begins: "These are the words of the Sun Suppiluliumas, the great king, the king of the Hatti land, the valiant, the favorite of the storm-god" (*The Ancient Near East*, vol. ii, p. 42).

historical prologue, in which the covenant initiator reviews the (good) relationship he or his forebears had with the vassal. The idea inherent in this section is that the initiating king is acting in a gracious manner; the treaty between Mursilis, Hittite king, and Duppi-Tessub has a prologue that in part says: "Aziras, your grandfather, Duppi-Tessub, rebelled against my father, but submitted again to my father. . . . When my father became a god [when Suppiluliumas died], and I seated myself on the throne of my father, Aziras behaved toward me just as he had behaved toward my father. . . . When your father died, in accordance with your father's word, I did not drop you."

the stipulations of the covenant, which consisted of that which the treaty maker expected of the vassal and was often worded in an "if . . . then" fashion; excerpts from the treaty between Mursilis and Duppi-Tessub include the following: "With my friend you shall be a friend, and with my enemy you shall be enemy. . . . If anyone utters words unfriendly to the king of Hatti land before you, Duppi-Tessub, you shall not withhold his name from the king."

provision for deposit of the treaty in the temple, which thereby made the covenant a matter for the gods to watch over, and for the public reading of it periodically; not all treaties spelled this out, although maybe it was understood.

the list of witnesses to the covenant typically included the deities of both countries and could be very exhaustive, so "that there was no god left that the vassal could appeal to for protection if he wanted to violate his solemn oath" (*Anchor Bible Dictionary*, Vol. I, p. 1181); the treaty between Mursilis and Duppi-Tessub included the following: "The sun-god of heaven, the sun-goddess of Arinna, the storm-god of heaven, . . . Ishtar of Nineveh, Ishtar of Hattarina, . . . Ninlil, the mountains, the rivers, the springs, . . . the clouds—let these be witnesses to this treaty and to the oath."

a list of blessings and curses, depending on the vassal's compliance with the stipulations of the treaty, most of which were seen to originate with the gods; for example, the treaty between Mursilis and Duppi-Tessub included the following: "Should Duppi-Tessub not honor these words of the treaty and the oath, may these gods of the oath destroy Duppi-Tessub together with his person, his wife, his son, his grandson, his house, his land and together with everything that he owns. But if Duppi-Tessub honors these words of the treaty and the oath that are inscribed on this tablet, may these gods of the oath protect him together with his person, his wife, his son, his grandson, his house, his country." A treaty made by King Esarhaddon of Assyria: "May Anu, king of the gods, rain upon all your houses disease, exhaustion, . . . sleeplessness, worries, ill health. May Sin, the luminary of heaven and earth, clothe you in leprosy. . . . May Shamash . . . take away your eyesight. . . . May Ninurta . . . fill the plain with your corpses, give your flesh to eagles and vultures to feed upon. . . . May Zarpanitu . . . eradicate your offspring and descendants from the land. . . . May Ea . . . give you deadly water to drink, and fill you with dropsy. . . . May Girra . . . burn your offspring and descendants." The list goes on and on.

Generally speaking, people executed such treaties by the slaying of a sacrificial animal. The inherent idea was that the same fate would await the party who violated the terms of the agreement.

What does all this have to do with studying the Bible? Well, in 1954 George Mendenhall, an especially creative (and sometimes eccentric) biblical scholar, wrote an essay that spelled out the similarities between these political ancient Near Eastern treaties and some of the covenants recorded in the Old Testament.

Mendenhall saw the giving of the Ten Commandments as described in the book of Deuteronomy (chapters 5 and following; see also Ex. 20ff.) as bearing close similarities to some of the Hittite treaties. In fact, Scripture calls the Decalogue itself a covenant (Deut. 4:13; see also 4:23; 5:2; 9:9, 11, 15; 29:1; 29:24, 25; Ex. 34:28). Notice the following parallels:

The covenant maker's identity is revealed: "I am YHWH your God" (Deut. 5:6).

A short historical prologue proclaims His graciousness to Israel: "I led you out of Egypt, out of the house of slavery" (see verse 6).

The stipulations follow: "You shall have no other gods before me. . . . You shall make no idols. . . . You shall not take My name in vain. . . . Remember to keep holy the seventh-day Sabbath. . . . You shall honor your father and mother. . . . You shall not steal" (see verses 7-21).

Provision for deposit of the document in the tabernacle: "And I will write on the tables the words that were in the first tables which thou brakest, and thou shalt put them in the ark" (Deut. 10:2; cf. verse 5; Ex. 25:21, 22; 40:20).

List of witnesses: "I call heaven and earth to witness against you this day," (Deut. 4:26).

List of curses and blessings: "Cursed be the man that maketh any graven or molten image. . . . Cursed be he that setteth light by his father or his mother." "Cursed be he that confirmeth not all the words of this law to do them. . . . Cursed shalt thou be in the city, and cursed shalt thou *be* in the field. . . . Cursed shall be the fruit of thy body, and the fruit of thy land, the increase of thy kine, and the flocks of thy sheep. Cursed shalt thou be when thou comest in, and cursed shalt thou be when thou goest out. The Lord shall send upon thee cursing, vexation, and rebuke . . . until thou be destroyed, and until thou perish quickly; . . . whereby thou hast forsaken me" (Deut. 27:15-26; 28:16-44). "Blessed shalt thou be in the city, and blessed shalt thou be in the field. Blessed shall be the fruit of thy body, and the fruit of thy ground, and the fruit of thy cattle, the increase of thy kine, and the flocks of thy sheep. . . . Blessed shalt thou be when thou comest in, and blessed shalt thou be when thou goest out. . . . The Lord shall command the blessing upon thee in thy storehouses, and in all that thou settest thine hand unto. . . . The Lord shall establish thee an holy people unto himself, as he hath sworn unto thee, if thou shalt keep the commandments of the Lord thy God, and walk in his ways. . . . And the Lord shall make thee the head, and not the tail; . . . if that thou hearken unto the commandments of the Lord thy God. . . . Thou shalt not go aside from any of the words which I command thee this day. . . to go after other gods to serve them" (Deut. 28:3-14).

The Old Testament mentions other covenants that God made with His people, beginning with Noah, and then with Abraham, and next with Isaac and Jacob. (Interestingly, God put His life on the line with the covenant He made with Abraham. His walking through the split carcasses of the sacrificial animals is an enactment of what would happen to Him if He did not fulfill His covenant.) The Sinai covenant underwent renewal several times. And later God made a covenant with David.

With this background in mind, from now on when you read about covenants in the Hebrew Bible and about grace in the New Testament you'll understand a little more about the dynamics behind these terms.

CHAPTER 7

Kinds of Communication—
Informative Discourse

Language—spoken or written—is a gift that most of us take for granted until . . .

Have you ever contracted a bad case of laryngitis? Or perhaps you know someone who had it? Then you know how frustrating it can be when you cannot communicate by speaking. Fortunately the condition is temporary. However, there are people who for whatever reason are mute. Maybe they were born without a larynx or with a defective one. Perhaps they were born profoundly deaf and never heard spoken language. Maybe they had to undergo surgery for throat cancer. Whatever the reason for lacking speech, such people—who otherwise are just like you and me—find their condition terribly frustrating.

Maybe you've been in a situation in which the people around you spoke a language foreign to you. When you hear them jabbering away among themselves, it sounds as though they are talking at a furious pace. You can't figure out where one word ends and the next begins. The truth is, however, that most people speak at pretty much the same rate of speed regardless of their native tongue. It just seems to untrained ears that they are talking lickety-split. Perhaps you may want to ask a simple question, such as "Where is the bathroom?" But you don't know the first thing about speaking Italian or Mandarin or Russian or . . .

Researchers have discovered that children can learn a language—even multiple languages—much more readily than can adults. Typically the younger children are when acquiring a language, the better their ability to speak it without an accent.

The same sort of frustrations we encounter when we hear spoken languages can arise with written language. For a long time in the history of the world people had no written language at all. Later in both Egypt (c. 3200 B.C.) and Mesopotamia (c. 3200 B.C.) someone invented picture writing. (Often scholars claim that the Mesopotamians edged out the Egyptians as the originators of writing.) The result is today called "hieroglyphics" for writing in Egypt and "cuneiform" for writing in Mesopotamia. Such ancient writing was still quite difficult because each word needed its own pictograph. Nonetheless, it was such an amazing breakthrough that both the Egyptians and the Mesopotamians spoke of writing as a divine gift.

At some point in time certain geniuses invented what we now call the alphabet. Scholars sometimes argue over where the alphabet first appeared, but for many years the consensus was that the first alphabet developed in the Sinai Peninsula not all that long before Moses led the Israelites through the same general area on the way to the Promised Land. The inventor or inventors of this alphabet turned Egyptian hieroglyphic pictures into letters, the picture standing for the first sound of a spoken word, a method called the acrophonic principle. A jagged line, for instance, portrayed water in hieroglyphics— MW . The inventor of the alphabet probably didn't know how to vocalize the Egyptian terminology for water (*nem mu*), but he knew how to pronounce the word in Canaanite—*mayim*. So the picture of water came to be uttered as *m*. Our English alphabet is actually a descendant of that Proto-Sinaitic alphabet, having evolved through the Canaanite, Hebrew, Greek, and Latin alphabets.

Modern alphabets, most of which have descended from the Proto-Sinaitic alphabet, contain varying numbers of letters. The Cambodian alphabet has 74 letters. The Armenian alphabet utilizes 39 letters. The alphabet with the fewest letters is that of the Rotokas language (spoken on Bougainville, an island to the east of Papua New Guinea), which contains only 11 letters.

In the ancient Near East most people couldn't read. That's why scribes held such an important role in society. They knew how to decipher the gift of the gods—writing. If a common, ordinary person needed a written document for whatever reason, he or she would find a scribe, who would—for a fee, of course—prepare the document. We cannot be certain that even kings were literate. Some may have been, but many were probably functionally illiterate. That's why royalty also employed scribes.

In this and the next five chapters we're going to explore language use. But we won't be dealing with the varying tongues that people speak. Instead, we're going to concentrate on how language—regardless of the tongue—gets used. In short, we'll be talking about how people employ it—with a focus on its result(s). For the sake of variety we'll be using as synonyms the words "language," "discourse," "communication," "utterance," and "speech." In other words, we'll use such words interchangeably.

We'll be looking at five types of communication—five ways we employ language, whether the tongue is French, Lakota, Hungarian, German, or . . . Since we use language to get things done, the intent behind the language is what we'll focus on. The kinds of discourse we'll be discussing in this chapter and the next are: (1) informative utterances, (2) cognitive discourse, (3) affective language, (4) performative communication, and (5) phatic speech. Examining each type separately, we will give secular examples as well as biblical ones of each kind of discourse.

Employing such an approach has helped me to understand what is "going on" when I read the Bible. I hope that you will find these distinctions helpful also.

Informative Language

The word "informative" first appeared in 1655. It means "imparting knowledge" (*Merriam-Webster's Collegiate Dictionary*, 11th edition). This type of discourse transmits *factual data* that can, theoretically at least, be independently verified—empirically confirmed. Such discourse provides what some might call "incorrigible data," that is, data that does not nor cannot change. When you use informative speech, you're providing pertinent information to others. Some traditional philosophers of language and speech insisted that it is really the only way people talk—making a statement. However, some philosophers, such as John Langshaw Austin (1911-1960), argued that we also use other kinds of utterances in everyday communication, which we'll be looking at in the following chapters.

The classic example of informative utterance is naming something. For example, suppose that you've been having a pain in your abdomen and that it has been getting worse. In fact, it has become so severe that even touching the area is excruciating. You make an appointment with your family physician. She performs a few tests and then says, "You have appendicitis." Dr. Williamson has just named your problem. It's now identified. And once it has been diagnosed, it can be treated. Ensuing surgery proves Dr. Williamson's informative utterance correct. Your appendix was very inflamed—actually, it was ready to rupture. But the surgeon removed it before you experienced serious complications.

Secular Examples of Informative Discourse

If I tell you that the church I attend is 5.3 miles from my house, that's an informative speech-act. I'm not sharing opinion or my emotional state, but am giving you hard data. Should you know the route that I take to church, you can use the odometer in your own car to prove or disprove my assertion.

We're all familiar with many other secular examples of informative communication. Articles reporting scientific research in the various professional journals represent informative discourse. Other scientists have "refereed" them so that readers of these professional journals will be justified in assuming that they are acquiring accurate data.

The maps in your road atlas are other examples of informative communication. You expect to be able to follow the routes printed across the page to the destination of your choice. And when you notice the color of the printed lines on the map, you get a pretty good inkling as to what kind of road you'll be driving on—a dirt road, an interstate, a two-lane road through town, etc.

Almanacs overflow with information about all sorts of places, persons, and things. You find there facts about the various nations of the world—the area in square miles, the population, the chief exports, the type of government, the national language(s), and other pertinent information, as well as sunrise and sunset tables; tide tables; economic tables; and all sorts of other detailed data. Want to know the population of Kansas City, Missouri? The almanac will have that information. Would you like to see a list of the major earthquakes throughout history? Check the almanac.

Encyclopedias contain similar information, although typically it is more in-depth than what you find in an almanac. Curious about Albert

Einstein? Look in the encyclopedia. It will give the date and place of his birth, a capsule history of his life, a list of his major accomplishments, a summary of his personal philosophy, and the date and place of his death. Seeking in-depth yet succinct information about Plato's philosophy? Turn to the encyclopedia, which will overflow with insights about his life and thought and writings.

Dictionaries—my favorite is the *Merriam-Webster's Collegiate Dictionary*—give the origin and meaning of words. The massive *Oxford English Dictionary's* volumes provide a history of each word along with examples of usage in the English language. Dictionaries represent another common example of informative discourse.

Corporate annual reports, balance sheets, and statements of consolidated income (verified independently, of course, by auditors) are yet another type of informative communication. Despite recent scandals in corporate America, what you find in these various business reports is supposed to be accurate.

Bird guides to North American birds consist pretty much entirely of informative discourse. Look in Roger Tory Peterson's *Field Guide to the Birds,* and you'll learn that a robin, which is between nine and 11 inches long, is a member of the thrush family. Identified in Latin terminology as *Turdus migratorius,* it ranges from Alaska and Canada south to Mexico and shows up in cities, towns, farmlands, lawns, shade trees, and forests. During the winter it stays close to trees with berries, which it eats.

Guides to North American flowering plants, guides to seashells, guides to rocks and minerals, guides to astronomy, guides to fungi, guides to club mosses, etc., all provide nature lovers with accurate information about the natural world around them.

Books for students, such as CliffsNotes and manuals that offer tutelage for taking ACT and SAT tests, represent still other examples of informative speech. Fodor, Moon, and other books on travel fall into the same category. The tour books that you get from AAA are another illustration of informative discourse.

Even Geiger counters, other gauges, scales, and measuring tapes provide useful measurement data for those who employ such instruments. Because, for example, the United States has a National Bureau of Standards and the National Institute of Standards and Technology, users of these various measuring devices assume that these devices provide reliable readings.

Certain styles of writing most often constitute informative discourse. Because with informative discourse we share information by talking about people, places, and things, essays as straightforward prose lend themselves most often to this type of communication. Writers using informative speech make frequent use of proper nouns and concrete nouns and employ forms of "to be" (is, are, was, were) frequently. Such writing does not always make for gripping reading, but sounds somewhat textbookish. Informative discourse makes use of the indicative mood (employed for stating a fact or asking a question) almost entirely, and typically it has a staccato cadence. Usually writers of informative communication use few metaphors and similes. Denotation (the definition of a word) is most important in informative speech.

Biblical Examples of Informative Discourse

It comes as a surprise to many people that the Bible does not contain much in the line of informative discourse. Such an observation can be especially troubling to those who think that they can use the Bible as a textbook for grammar, science, math, history, etc. That is generally a misuse of Scripture. As Galileo is reputed to have argued (or was it really Cardinal Baronius?): "The Holy Scriptures are intended to teach men how to go to heaven, not how the heavens go."

"But wait!" I can hear you protest. "Where else can we get information about Abraham? Where else can we learn about his wife Sarah, his wife Hagar, his wife Keturah, and his concubines? Where else can we find out about Abraham's children—Isaac and Ishmael, as well as Zimram, Jokshan, Medan, Midian, Ishbak, and Shuah?"

Yes, you're right. These are examples of informative speech. But the fact is that Scripture has preserved such accounts not to satisfy our curiosity about the forefather of the Jews but to help us spiritually. "Now all these things happened unto them for ensamples: and they are written for our admonition" (1 Cor. 10:11).

Encyclopedias and almanacs, for instance, have one chief purpose—the sharing of data about persons, places, and things. Not so with Scripture. It is not an encyclopedia of Old Testament patriarchs. Nor is it an almanac of New Testament facts. We may find in its pages information that satisfies our thirst for trivia. However, God didn't inspire the writers of the Bible to pen a compendium for players of a Bible trivia board game.

The Abraham stories have a magnificent purpose behind them. They helped the ancient Hebrews keep in touch with their spiritual roots. Reading about Father Abraham was supposed to help them learn to be like him—faithful to the God of heaven. Emulating Abraham's admirable lifestyle and eschewing his dishonorable behavior, they were to use him as their point of reference when it came to spiritual and ethical matters. When they said, "Abraham is our father," it should have implied "Like father, like son." It should have meant that their daily lives compared favorably with his.

If we assume that the author of the Abraham stories preserved them solely for the sake of the information they contained, then we will not be able to read the stories productively. The person who recorded those events had an ulterior motive in mind. It was not history for its own sake, but history with a bias—history interpreted, history in which God as well as humans are involved in the act.

"The writers of the Old Testament were interested seldom in history in our sense, but in matters of faith and theology" (Gene Tucker, *The Old Testament and the Historian*, pp. iii, iv). Edgar Krentz wrote something similar: "The Bible narrates history for a kerygmatic (or edificatory, or doxological) purpose" (*The Historical-Critical Method*, p. 72).

Scripture does contain other examples of informative discourse. Consider, for instance, those devastatingly boring genealogies. "Shem was an hundred years old, and began Arphaxad two years after the flood: and Shem lived after he begat Arphaxad five hundred years, and begat sons and daughters. And Arphaxad lived five and thirty years, and begat Salah . . ." (Gen. 11:10-12ff.). Some of those genealogies seem to go on for ever and ever!

Yet even then we must recognize that when dealing with biblical genealogies, we are not reading mere family trees. Those family trees have been shaped and sculpted—much like bonsai trees or topiary. Comparing the various genealogies with each other, we sometimes find that entire generations are missing. Maybe all the genealogies have been pruned. We simply don't know. We do know, however, that the genealogy of Jesus given in Matthew has indeed been carefully shaped. Each branch of the family tree has exactly 14 generations—even though the evidence in the Old Testament shows that there were more than just 14 generations in the branches. And so the book of Matthew omits some names.

Here are a few more examples of informative communication within the Bible. "Abraham weighed to Ephron the silver, . . . four hundred shekels of silver. ... And the field of Ephron, which was in Machpelah, which was before Mamre, the field, and the cave which was therein, and all the trees that were in the field, that were in all the borders round about, were made sure unto Abraham for a possession in the presence of the children of Heth, before all that went in at the gate of his city. And after this, Abraham buried Sarah his wife in the cave of the field of Machpelah before Mamre: the same is Hebron in the land of Canaan" (Gen. 23:16-19).

"Against him came up Nebuchadnezzar king of Babylon" (2 Chron. 36:6).

"Now in the fifteenth year of the reign of Tiberius Caesar, Pontius Pilate being governor of Judaea, and Herod being tetrarch of Galilee, and his brother Philip tetrarch of Ituraea and of the region of Trachonitis, and Lysanias the tetrarch of Abilene" (Luke 3:1).

"There they crucified him" (Luke 23:33).

As we saw previously, naming someone is also a use of informative discourse. And we find some of that in the Bible too. "And Adam called his wife's name Eve" (Gen. 3:20).

"And it came to pass, as her soul was in departing, (for she died) that she called his name Benoni: but his father called him Benjamin" (Gen. 35:18).

"He shall be called John" (Luke 1:60). "Thou shalt call his name JESUS: for he shall save his people from their sins. . . . And [Joseph] called his name JESUS" (Matt. 1:21-25).

Frequently in Scripture when someone gives a name to someone else, the biblical authors include an etymology given to explain the name. Many times, however, these etymologies are what scholars call "folk etymologies." In a technical linguistic sense, those explanations for the meaning of the proper noun are inaccurate. Therefore, they are not really informative speech, although they look like that. Rather they are examples of cognitive discourse, which we shall discuss in the next chapter.

Examples of some folk etymologies given in Scripture are the following. "Therefore is the name of it called Babel; because the Lord did there confound the language of all the earth: and from thence did the Lord scatter them abroad upon the face of all the earth" (Gen. 11:9). The word "Babel" technically means "Gate of God" (in Canaanite) or "Gate of the Gods" (in Mesopotamian), but its *sound* is reminiscent of the Hebrew word that means confusion. (*Babel* is confused with *balal*.) Furthermore, the old word "Babel" is very close to our English word "babble."

You've probably heard it said that the name of the city Jerusalem has something to do with the word "peace," and hence Jerusalem is the city of peace. This popular explanation confuses the ancient Near Eastern god known as Salem with the Hebrew word that means peace—*shalom*. The connotation of peace does not rightfully belong with the proper noun Jerusalem. The word "Jerusalem" has its origins in paganism.

Hebrew scholars tell us that popular etymologies are often based on puns and not on solid linguistic connection or evidence. So even though the simple explanation of proper nouns in the Bible may sound like informative discourse, it really is not, because the data passed along to readers is not technically and linguistically correct. (That does not mean that the message that the Bible is teaching through such plays on words is wrong. It is truth presented in a way that we are not as familiar with in our modern, scientifically oriented world.)

Let me reiterate. Informative language itself is either true or false. If you buy Fodor's *France*, you consider it to be accurate. When the book says that the Louvre is open from 9:45 a.m. to 5:00 p.m., you assume that you can visit the famous art museum between those two times. And you have every right to expect the data given to be accurate. That's what informative speech is all about.

There can be, I suppose, false informative communication—discourse that passes itself off as sharing accurate data but that is really a collection of falsehoods or pseudo-facts (if I may use that self-contradictory term). If that which purports to contain informative language actually provides false data, readers have every right to become outraged and criticize the author and publisher. On the other hand, when the purpose of a piece of communication is other than informative (suppose that it is cognitive discourse instead), then accuracy of each individual data is not the main point. If the author gets some of the facts bungled, you don't feel cheated or lied to, and you don't get outraged. Accuracy of details is not an issue, because the communicator was not engaged in informative discourse.

This understanding is crucial when it comes to Scripture. One day my phone rang, and May was on the other end of the line. A woman with whom she had been studying the Bible had clipped a letter to the editor from the Nashville *Tennessean* and had showed it to May. The writer of the letter had recounted some contradictions in what is called the Synoptic Gospels—Matthew, Mark, and Luke.

"What about this?" May's friend asked her.

And May was floored. She had no answer, although her first impulse was to deny the allegations in the letter to the editor. So she phoned me, and I freely admitted that the letter writer was correct in his observations. "There *are* discrepancies," I told her, "in the Gospel accounts."

"But how do you explain this?" she wanted to know.

How? I began by stating that we must be honest with the data. We must not allow our love for the Bible to blind us to the facts of the case. That would be religious infatuation, not love. The facts indicate that the Gospel writers sometimes conflict with each other in certain minor details.

For example, precisely what did the sign say that Pilate had nailed atop Jesus' cross? The Gospel writers can't seem to agree on the precise wording. Exactly how many demoniacs at Gadara did Jesus exorcise? Did Jesus heal blind Bartimaeus on the way *into* Jericho or on the way *out*? We could give other examples.

If the Gospel writers had set out to give us a biographical and chronological account of the life and works of Jesus of Nazareth, then we would feel—and rightfully so—shortchanged to discover these discrepancies. But the genre known as Gospel is not identical with that of today's historical biographies. The Gospel authors didn't set out to share data about Jesus' miracles or sayings merely to keep us informed. They didn't write an encyclopedia or almanac entry. The Gospels are not an example of the informative use of language even though we sometimes use the expression "Gospel truth" to refer to accurate or truthful data. (We'll talk more about the implications of "truth" later.)

John explains the purpose behind his Gospel—and undoubtedly the same purpose lay behind the other Gospels. "But these are written, that ye might believe that Jesus is the Christ, the Son of God; and that believing ye might have life through his name" (John 20:31). Those words imply that the biblical authors did not write the Gospels as informative discourse. The disciple—and the other Gospel writers—had a religious response in mind when they wrote. Their goal was to transform lives, not just provide encyclopedia entries.

It took May a little thoughtful contemplation before she could accept this concept.

We find the same thing in the Old Testament. If I thought that the Bible were a biology textbook, I'd feel upset when I read that snakes eat dust (Gen. 3:14), that birds and insects have four legs (Lev. 11:20-23), and that bats are birds (Deut. 14:18). Or if the Bible were a textbook in math, I'd feel gypped to discover that the value of pi in Chronicles (2 Chron 4:2) is exactly 3.00—when the Egyptians had already worked out pi to several decimal places.

Biology and math textbooks are examples of informative communication. I have a right to get upset if the information they contain is false, but most sections of Scripture are not examples of informative discourse, so the accuracy of the minute details is not an issue. However, it would be a serious deficiency on the part of Scripture if the biblical text claimed to be informative communication in the strict modern sense. Since it has greater goals than that, I don't get a troubled mind over such little side issues. One's expectations of the text must be in keeping with the exact use of the language involved.

CHAPTER 8

Kinds of Communication— Cognitive Discourse

C ognitive" is another big word, one we don't normally use every day. Although I'd heard of the word, it actually became part of my vocabulary after I had read the book *Theory of Cognitive Dissonance,* by Leon Festinger. The book explained that sometimes evidence that piles upon evidence can challenge a long-held belief. When that happens, our mind struggles to cope with two competing belief systems, a process called "cognitive dissonance."

When cognitive dissonance reaches the point where it truly becomes painful to the psyche, the person comes up with ways to resolve the dissonance, or conflict, plaguing the mind. Someone may abandon the previous belief entirely, accepting the new concept. Or one might try to rationalize that both the old and the new beliefs are correct but are paradoxes that we need to hold in tension. Another might decide that while certain parts of the old belief were valid, other parts of it were not.

Cognitive Language

After several oblique references to cognitive discourse in the previous chapter, it's time to turn our attention to it. This use of the word describes not mental dissonance but a way to use language. The word "cognitive" first surfaced in 1586 and describes "conscious intellectual activity," such as thinking and reasoning (*Merriam-Webster's Collegiate Dictionary*, 11th edition). With cognitive communication we share ideas—thoughts and concepts and opinions.

When we employ cognitive speech, we resort to using forms of the verb "to be." We also often preface cognitive language with such expressions as "I believe," "I think," "It seems to me," or "In my opinion." Writing that provides cognitive discourse is generally more abstract than informative discourse, even though the two may sometimes resemble each other. Authors often resort to the subjunctive mood, such as "It might be . . ."

That which we share through cognitive language we are usually not able to verify independently through empirical means. Cognitive presentations often use a lot of metaphors, similes, and other figures of speech. You may find frequent comparisons in material that is cognitive in nature and purpose. Sometimes we might find cognitive discourse hard to follow.

Cognitive language should be logical, but it deals with beliefs, and it's easy to argue over beliefs because of the lack of warrant (confirmation) from empirical proof to use in settling a matter. We use cognitive discourse to share theoretical constructs—ideas that we have in our head but that we cannot support or prove beyond the shadow of a doubt.

Cognitive speech presses into service deductive and inductive reasoning, for instance. And the conclusions from these two forms of logic—especially from inductive logic—may be the only evidence for or against the ideas presented through cognitive communication. Ideally, cognitive discourse will abide by the canons of sound logic, but sometimes logic can take us only so far in our quest for understanding.

Some of us are better than others at cognitive communication. That doesn't make some of us superior to others. It may be simply a matter of personal makeup—maybe even a matter of how our brains are "wired."

Generally speaking, the broader our vocabulary and that of the recipients, the more precision we can bring to our attempts to share our concepts with others. We all have probably known small children who used the word "kitty" for any four-legged animal. Dogs were kitties. Squirrels were kitties. Skunks were kitties. Why, cows and horses were just big kitties! But as those childrens' vocabularies grew and their perception sharpened, they soon began classifying mammals into more precise categories. If the language that children are learning doesn't engender a wide vocabulary for animals, then those growing children will not learn how to differentiate among mammals as precisely as they might otherwise do. Perception just might get locked into a relatively simplistic and limited outlook. Personally, I can distinguish between a Bactrian camel and a dromedary (Arabian) camel. Some people may not discern the difference. But the Arabic language of past generations, I'm told, had numerous words applying to the beast that we call a dromedary.

Additionally, once we begin classifying objects, we (1) perceive more thoroughly those things that we have classified and have given names to and (2) fail to see beyond those things that we have named—the use of informative language.

Finally, many of us limit our differentiation to polar opposites: good or bad, black or white, cold or hot, high or low, wide or narrow, many or few. Such a dualistic perspective is very restrictive. We can achieve more precision by increasing our perceptual differentiation. Naming and drawing fine distinctions may be part of informative language, but it can also aid in our own cognitive communication.

However, abstruse thought allows cognitive discourse to come into its own. It gives us the capacity to speak about love, faith, hope, awe, knowledge, truth, beauty, nothingness, infinity, etc. The ancient Greeks especially taught us how to think and talk abstractly. The mental efforts of the great Greek philosophers have left us with an amazingly rich heritage. Socrates, Plato, Aristotle, and others—we owe them a great debt.

We see the influence of such great philosophers in the New Testament. Paul's arguments often revolve around such abstract concepts as justice, righteousness, love, faith, belief, obedience, law, sin, unrighteousness, and unbelief. In fact, his philosophizing at times got so obscure that Peter had to admit that in Paul's writings "are some things hard to be understood" (2 Peter 3:16).

In the Old Testament, though, we find little in the way of abstract thinking. The Hebrew mind owed very little to the ancient Greek thinkers. So instead of finding a lot of philosophical rationalization in the Old Testament, we encounter a wide range of concrete imagery. Now, don't misunderstand. I'm not implying that the Hebrew Bible writers could not or did not use cognitive language. They did, but their cognitive speech was much more concrete than that which we find in the New Testament. In the Old Testament, ideas come to us via pictures and stories and rituals. As a result, when reading the Old Testament we often assume that we're encountering informative discourse. In reality, however, we're face to face with cognitive communication but in a slightly different form.

The Hebrew Bible is not a theological treatise on sin, guilt, atonement, and cleansing, for example, as some of Paul's writings were. Instead, in its pages we read about a sanctuary, about priests, about animal sacrifices, and about ritual burnings and sprinkling of blood. Moses didn't speculate, as do modern Christians, about the big bang that started the universe and how matter can turn into energy and vice versa. Instead, he wrote: "In the beginning God created. . . . And God said . . . : and it was so" (Gen. 1:1ff.). Rather than declaring, as John did, that God is love, David wrote a poem that began with the words "The Lord is my shepherd; I shall not want" (Ps. 23:1).

Secular Examples of Cognitive Discourse

We'll talk more about this a little later. But now it's time to consider some contemporary examples of cognitive discourse.

In my personal library is a set of large tomes called *Encyclopedia of Philosophy*. It has a significant amount of informative communication (facts about the various philosophers, for instance), as an encyclopedia would. But it also includes a lot of cognitive discourse—explanations about the philosophical ideas of the various great thinkers. Some of the material in these volumes can be quite challenging to understand. In fact, some of it is way over my head. My point here is that these volumes contain a lot of cognitive communication.

More easily understood is a paperback book that I own titled *Philosophy Made Simple*. That's almost an oxymoron, because philosophical thought can be quite difficult to comprehend at times. However, here again is an example of cognitive discourse because the book helps readers understand the ideas taught by the great philosophers. But the volume also contains a smattering of informative discourse.

Mortimer Adler in his book *How to Think About God* tries to employ pure logic to demonstrate the existence of God. His use of cognitive discourse makes fascinating reading—fascinating, that is, when I can follow his abstractions. C. S. Lewis in *Mere Christianity*, a much more easily understood book, presents what has come to be known as the moral argument to buttress belief in God's existence. *Mere Christianity* thus offers another example of cognitive language.

Anselm, archbishop of Canterbury and master theologian who lived from 1033 or 1034 to 1109, wrote a theological treatise called *Proslogion*. In his classic work Anselm came up with a very interesting definition of God. God, he insisted, is "that than which no greater can be conceived." This line of reasoning has come to be known as the "ontological argument" for God's existence. And here we find another instance of cognitive discourse.

A relatively recent phenomenon is the existence of chat rooms on the Internet—forums for people to discuss, exchange, and challenge ideas on any number of topics. Examples of cognitive communication fill such chat rooms.

For a number of years it was my privilege to write articles for magazines that presented doctrinal concepts with individuals of other religious or nonreligious background. When talking about God and biblical doctrines, I was using a form of cognitive communication.

For six years I served as a pastor in Massachusetts, and nearly every week I had to preach a new sermon. Sermons afford another example of cognitive speech. Talks given at weddings and funerals also embody cognitive language.

In the early 1960s the pastor of the Atlantic Union College church declared war on the English Department. Why? Because students in the English and American literature classes were required to read fiction as part of the course requirements. He was neither the first nor the last to raise an objection to fiction. Many others have felt that Christian educational institutions should ban fiction because it is not true. As a result, a number of years ago the Department of Education of my church prepared a paper that addressed the same issue, arguing that certain types of fiction were permissible.

During the 1980s the book editors at the Review and Herald Publishing Association (in consultation with the magazine editors) prepared a brochure titled "When Fiction Is True." It pointed out the fact that authors of even "true" stories often used creative writing techniques, such as including events that never took place, to keep the story line moving or making up (reconstructing) conversation to add realism to the story. Furthermore, the brochure argued, forbidding fiction because it is not factual misses the point. Certain literary pieces that can be categorized as fiction actually portray truth even though the story itself may not be factual in every (or any) detail. The publishing houses exist to produce "truth-filled literature," and fiction can be truth-filled. Strictly speaking, facticity and truthfulness are not necessarily the same thing.

On the one hand, it is possible for a story to be completely factual but not worthy of publication because it distorts reality since the factual incident reported is not typical of real life for the majority of people. On the other hand, a story may be "made up" in the author's imagination yet provide a truthful observation into real life. In the latter situation the writing is cognitive discourse. A story need not consist solely of informative discourse. Indeed, the lack of factuality in a narrative does not necessitate that it is distorting real life. Indeed, it may be telling the truth about human existence.

In fact, the Bible does contain fiction as cognitive discourse—not a lot, but some. We find the story about the trees wanting to elect a king (Judges 9:8-15); Isaiah portrayed the king of Babylon going down into Sheol, where the deceased taunted him (14:4-16); Ezekiel told a fictional story about God's happening upon an abandoned baby girl, whom He adopted, later fell in love with, and married when she became a teenager, but who turned out to be an unfaithful lover (16:3-63); Jesus employed the story of the rich man and Lazarus, clearly a fictitious parable (Luke 16:20-30); in fact, many biblical scholars consider almost all of Jesus' parables as a form of fiction; and the books of Daniel and Revelation contains images of strange beasts constructed from various animal parts—depictions that can be only fictitious (Dan. 7; 8; Rev. 5-13).

Biblical Examples of Cognitive Discourse

In Scripture we find a lot of cognitive discourse. In fact, I'd hazard a guess that most of the Bible consists of cognitive communication—with other forms of discourse scattered throughout or blended with the cognitive discourse.

In Genesis 1-3 we read about the creation of Planet Earth, the creation of life on the planet, the establishment of the Garden of Eden, the making of Adam and Eve, and the entrance of sin. It's easy to think of these chapters as informative speech, but I'd like to suggest that we regard them as examples of cognitive communication. We're reading about things that we cannot independently and empirically verify. Those stories tell us about theoretical constructs—spiritual ideas. That doesn't necessarily mean that what we read here is less "real" than what we find in an almanac. Rather, it means that we have moved from the realm of knowledge with its informative discourse (data that we can logically or empirically prove) to the realm of belief with its cognitive discourse (understandings that we accept by faith).

A favorite biblical passage in the New Testament is John 3:16. It is a wonderful verse of Scripture, and for many years I have been working on a book that opens up the meanings I find in just that single verse. However, when anyone talks about God, love, belief, salvation, and everlasting life, we're in the realm of cognitive language.

Most philosophers of religion, including those who believe in God, admit that we cannot empirically or logically prove the existence of YHWH, the biblical God. Even if Mortimer Adler, for example, succeeded in demonstrating through logic alone the existence of God (as he believed that he had done in *How to Think About God*), he himself admitted at the end of the book that he had not proved the existence of YHWH, the God portrayed in the Old Testament. And it doesn't take a genius to recognize that we cannot prove (without doubt) the activities of someone whose very existence we cannot prove (without doubt).

In the Bible we find two similar yet different kinds of "prophetic" utterances. Scholars call one type "prophecy" and the other "apocalyptic." There are numerous distinctions between the two, but for our present discussion I'll mention only one.

According to prophecy, God's people were suffering because they were bad. Read the Old Testament prophets, and you find them asserting again and again that Israel had broken covenant with God. By forsaking YHWH, they had become like an adulterous wife. They had oppressed the poor, namely, the widows and orphans. As a result of their evil ways, they were suffering—rain had been withheld, crops had withered, and foreign nations (Assyria and Babylon) had invaded the land and taken away God's people as prisoners of war.

According to apocalyptic, however, God's people were suffering because they were good. The cosmic powers of evil were attacking God's people because His people had been faithful to their God. Evil people hate good people. As a result of their righteous lives, God's people experienced persecution. But evil never really triumphs—at least not in the end. And so the persecution of the righteous would not last forever. The devil and his cohorts will not have the last word. God will. Persecution will not run its full course but will be cut short . . . and God will rescue His good people.

If it were possible to see immaterial spiritual things, we might be able to decide which perspective was right and which was wrong—if we must choose between those two options that face us in prophecy and apocalyptic. We could, then, perhaps be in the realm of informative discourse. But we can't pull aside the veil that separates our material world from the spiritual world. And so we cannot without a doubt say why any of God's people are suffering. Thus when it comes to prophecy and apocalyptic, we're in the realm of cognitive—not informative—discourse.

The biblical apocalyptic book of Revelation, the last book in the Bible, includes many numbers in its prophecies. Roy Naden has pointed out that we should not understand the numbers in literal terms but rather should see them as symbolic, which means we're here dealing with cognitive discourse and not informative communication. I think that he is correct.

Here's one example. Revelation 11:9, 11, refers to a period of persecution that would last for three and a half days. There are at least three different ways of interpreting this number—all of which recognize this passage as cognitive discourse. The first way of understanding the number would be to think of a time of persecution that would last for 3.5 literal 24-hour days. Yet another approach would be to use the day-for-a-year principle, which calculates out to be 3.5 years of 360 days each, or 1,260 days. However, a third way to interpret this number would be to recognize that biblical apocalyptic considers the number seven to be a perfect number—a number of completion. Therefore, three and a half is a broken seven, which thus symbolizes a period of persecution, but a length of time in which persecution doesn't reach its final conclusion—utter destruction. Rather, this period of persecution is only half of perfection, meaning that it falls short of completion.

Earlier we spoke about genealogies in the Bible. We noted that these family trees were often trimmed—like bonsai or topiary plants. Scripture offers good evidence that in some genealogies the biblical writer omitted several generations. I used genealogies as examples of informative discourse. But then I waffled. Why? It may be that genealogies, despite their appearance of being informative speech, might more accurately be classified as cognitive speech. Or perhaps they are a blend of both types of discourse—informative and cognitive.

While people expected that their genealogies would contain accurate data (informative communication), that does not seem to have been their chief function. Let me explain.

In the biblical world, honor and shame, as we noted in chapter 4, were the foundational concepts of society. "Honor is the value of a person in his or her own eyes (that is, one's claim to worth) *plus* that person's value in the eyes of his or her social group" (Bruce J. Malina, *The New Testament World*, p. 27).

You may recall that people were born with one kind of honor (anthropologists call it "ascribed honor"). Such honor depended upon the extended kinship system within which they were born. Additionally, they could obtain more honor (anthropologists call it "acquired honor") by their noble behavior, which could include winning—in public—arguments with their peers (as we saw previously, anthropologists label such activity "challenge and riposte"). People worked hard at maintaining a bank account, so to speak, of honor and at avoiding any accumulation of shame, which could deplete that savings account of honor.

Furthermore, people in that society viewed "wealth" differently from the way we Westerners see it. They believed in what is called "limited good." Only a finite and fixed amount of honor, wealth, and land existed. If Mr. A gained some honor, wealth, or land, then Mr. Z lost some honor, wealth, or land. Let's think about ownership of land for a moment. This patriarchal and patrilineal society transferred land from father to son. And land was important to own because it was the source of all food and wealth and most people barely subsisted in that culture. Owning land to farm could make the difference between leading an almost comfortable life or just barely eking out an existence because someone else had the land.

Now you can see why genealogies served an important function. A genealogy could indicate to people not only the value of one's ascribed honor, but also property ownership. So genealogies played an important role in society, and we should probably regard them as more cognitive discourse than informative communication.

In the Old Testament we read about clean and unclean animals, people, and things. If we take these discussions literally, then we must assume that frogs have more dirt on them than do sheep. Yet frogs are always bathing! They live in water, whereas sheep's wool gets matted with mud and fecal material. Also we would have to assume that frogs transmit more disease to humans than do chickens. But have you ever heard of hundreds of thousands of frogs being killed because they're host for a flu that could kill hundreds of thousands of humans—Asian frog flu?

Here's a suggestion for you to think about. All the talk about clean and unclean animals (and clothing and walls and people) in Leviticus is really *not* informative speech at all but cognitive communication instead. Leviticus 11 is not a primer in veterinary medicine or human pathology or epidemiology. The idea of clean and unclean was a figure of speech, so to speak. It was a spiritual metaphor to help the Hebrew people get their minds around such abstract ideas as moral and spiritual holiness, so that they could conform to the command "Ye shall be holy; for I am holy" (Lev. 11:44; cf. "For thou art an holy people unto the Lord thy God" [Deut. 7:6]). We miss the point when we literalize the discussion and think that unclean versus clean referred exclusively to physical or physiological conditions.

Think a moment about dirt. Dirt is matter that is out of place. At the beach sand under the soles of your feet is delightful, and you curl your toes in it. But on the bathroom floor sand feels repulsive. It's dirt! So you grab a broom and immediately sweep it up, throwing out that offensive dirt. (You likely won't even use the word "sand" for the grit on the bathroom floor!) Then there's egg. The omelet on your plate at breakfast is food, and thus clean. The egg that you leave on your plate after you've satisfied your appetite suddenly becomes garbage. And the egg stuck on your face when you arrive at work is dirt.

Matter that is out of place is unclean. But matter that remains in its proper place is clean. It all depends on how we structure the universe about us and how faithfully we maintain the proper distinctions. By the same token, that which did not fit into the thought patterns of the Hebrews were anomalies, and they came to represent that which was un-worthy, unholy—that which was out of place in God's cosmos. Frogs, for instance, were not fish, yet they lived in ponds as fish do. Yet they had no fins and scales like fish. Thus frogs were an anomaly—out of place, so to speak—and so were unclean. Bats looked like mice and had fur (if one got that close to them), but they flew in the air like birds with feathers. Again they were an anomaly, and so were unclean.

In the Old Testament world of the Hebrew people the term *unclean* implied a pollution that was more abstract than mud and germs. *Unclean* implied a special kind of defilement that violated the essential unity and order of creation. Thus it became a practical metaphor for the unity and sanctity of people who were to be holy because their God, YHWH, was holy. Thus the language about "clean" and "unclean" was not informative communication but cognitive discourse. While it sometimes had aspects of health and hygiene, it really involved issues of religious education, of abstract ideas (theoretical constructs) of wholeness: holiness.

Cognitive discourse often resorts to metaphors to help us to better understand God. Yet at the same time this very imagery—if taken as pure informative language—can distort His reality, especially when we take them literally. Dr. John Harvey Kellogg wrote a book called *The Living Temple*. In it he took literally some of the biblical metaphors. The resulting discussion in his book sounds rather ridiculous to our ears today, but Dr. Kellogg was completely serious.

Isaiah described God as He "who hath measured the waters in the hollow of his hand, and meted out heaven with a span" (40:12). Overwhelmed by that imagery, Dr. Kellogg wrote: "A hand large enough to hold the waters of the earth in its hollow would be as large as the earth itself. . . . A span great enough to mete out even the earthly heavens would cover at least 9,000 square miles. Try to form a conception of a hand of such proportions; when outstretched, the distance from the tip of the thumb to the tip of the little finger would be 9,000 miles. The height of a person is nine times the length of the span, so the height of a being with such proportions must be at least 81,000 miles. It is just as easy to conceive of a person filling all space as of a person having a height equaling ten times the diameter of the earth" (pp. 32, 33).

Next Dr. Kellogg dealt with the passage that "it is [God] that sitteth upon the circle of the earth" (40:22). Commented Kellogg: "This great being is represented as sitting on the circle of the earth. The orbit of the earth is nearly two hundred million miles in diameter" (p. 33). You know where he was headed, don't you? He was about to speculate on the size of God's derriere.

What's the problem with Dr. Kellogg's reasoning? Why does it sound so ridiculous to us? The answer is quite simple. Taking biblical figures of speech literally, he interpreted the analogies in a wooden manner. He acted as though these statements were informative language, when in fact they were cognitive discourse.

Once we recognize that much of the Bible consists of cognitive language, we will be spared much of the grief and confusion that plague those who think they must take such language at face value. When we confuse scriptural cognitive discourse with informative communication, we have set ourselves up for confusion and ultimate disillusionment.

In informative language the issue at stake is whether or not the data is *factual*. But cognitive language, when used properly, has the virtue of being *rational*. That is, does the language get across concepts in a rational manner? Does the metaphor, if one is used, help us think more clearly? In other words, the data of an example in cognitive discourse may be false as in a fable in which nonhuman entities speak. (Think of Aesop's fables or Jotham's story of the trees electing a king in Judges 9:7-15.) The issue is not whether animals or trees talk but whether the illustration of talking objects gets across rationally the concept that the communicator seeks to share.

And so the story Jesus told about the rich man and Lazarus and Abraham's bosom (Luke 16:20-30) should not perplex us. It is yet another example of cognitive speech. Jesus was trying to get across a specific idea. The issue at stake is not whether the dead live on in torment or in Abraham's bosom after their demise. Factuality of specific data is not at issue here. Rather the point is whether Jesus, by adopting and adapting a familiar motif, got His point across to His audience. Cognitive discourse should lead to rationality and not to fallacy.

We need to discuss three more kinds of communication in relationship to Scripture. We shall do that in the following chapters.

CHAPTER 9

Kinds of Communication—
Performative Discourse

Do you know how many languages people speak around the world? Not all authorities agree, because (1) the data is not necessarily complete, (2) languages can die with the last person speaking that language, and (3) linguists sometimes dispute what constitutes a separate language. Should, for instance, a dialect be considered a separate language? Is Canadian French a different language from Parisian French? Is Castilian Spanish a different language from Mexican Spanish?

Yourdictionary.com says that the earth has 6,800 spoken languages. *Encyclopedia Americana* (2003 ed., vol. 16, p. 731) gives the number as 6,500. *World Book Encyclopedia* (2001 ed., vol. 12, p. 62) suggests 6,000 languages. According to the *Guinness Book of World Records*, people in Papua New Guinea speak the largest number of languages in a given country—869. How many of the following languages have you heard of? Swahili. Kannada. Twi. Ainu. Tagalog. Hokan. Yupik. Gilyak. Tlingit.

However, we are not concerned with specific languages in these chapters. Rather, we're discussing certain ways in which we use language—regardless of whatever mother tongue we speak—and how such forms of discourse relate to Bible study.

Performative Language

The spell checker in your word processing software might flag the word "performative," but it really is a legitimate word, although it is of relatively recent origin. First used in 1955, it refers to "an expression . . . that constitutes the performance of the specified act by virtue of its utterance" (*Merriam-Webster's Collegiate Dictionary*, 11th edition). That's not the most lucid definition I've ever read, but as we get into our discussion of performative discourse, the meaning will become clearer.

Performative discourse is language in work clothes. It expresses what you want done, but more than that—your having spoken the "word," the action follows. Performative language deals with volition—yours and ultimately others'.

Typically performative communication is not lengthy. Most of the time it's quite short and terse. In fact, sometimes we will employ only a single word, as when a sentry shouts, "Halt!" Performative discourse often uses the imperative mood—commands. Performative utterances ultimately specify some kind of action—even if the action is only hinted at or mentioned obliquely.

The magician was putting on a program at Atlantic Union College. My dad was a ministerial student there, and the magician was—of all people!—the college president. I was about 5 or 6 years old at the time and sat wide-eyed near the front of the auditorium as G. Eric Jones performed his tricks.

Suddenly his eyes focused on me, and he asked me to come onto the stage. After proper introductions, he proceeded to pierce my right elbow with a trick ice pick, after which he pumped my left arm. While I repeated the appropriate magical expression, milk flowed from my right elbow, through a funnel, and into a pitcher. And it was real milk! The magician offered me some, but I demurred, so he demonstrated that it was the real thing by drinking the milk himself. Then Dr. Jones gave me an orange, which he materialized from a hat, and sent me back to sit with my parents.

Throughout the next week my playmates and I uttered "magic words" over sundry objects. Oh, how we wanted to replicate the magic that we had watched that previous Saturday night. But alas, our magic words lacked effectiveness! We were, of course, too young and naive to recognize that the "magic" didn't reside in the words but in the gimmickry that the college president had at his disposal.

Words, I understand today, don't have any mysteriously magical power. *Abracadabra* means nothing. *Hocus pocus* is powerless. Yet even today some adults—who really should know better—will say something and then, to assure that what they uttered won't come to pass, repeat "knock on wood" and rap their knuckles on any piece of nearby wood—I suppose to break the spell. (Scholars have not found any authoritative explanation for the origin of this expression.)

Primitive peoples—like small children—often believe that words possess magic power. And so they show great care about what they verbalize. This has often been especially true of proper nouns. "The magic attitude toward personal names requires that these names not be taken in vain or, in some cases, not even uttered" (John C. Condon, Jr., *Semantics and Communication*, 2nd ed., p. 108).

In ancient Egypt—as among a number of Australian and New Zealand tribespeople—everyone had at least two names: the one by which one was addressed, but also the real name, which the individual kept a closely guarded secret. The Masai people of Africa refuse to repeat the name of a dead person, lest they bring death upon themselves. Often to name a person or know a person's name implies having power over that individual. That's why exorcists try to learn the name of the demon they intend to cast out—so that they can gain control over the demon. For example, as soon as Jesus learned the name of the demon possessing the Gadarene demoniac, He cast it out.

Secular Examples of Performative Discourse

All this sounds very primitive to us. We Westerners know that words don't have any inherent power. Yet millions of Roman Catholics truly believe that when the priest consecrates the "Host" by saying, "*Hoc est corpus meum*," the wafer transubstantiates into the actual body of our Lord and the wine turns into His real blood. It's as though the Latin expression "Hoc est corpus meum"—"This is My body"—has magical or supernatural power. In fact, this incantation is most likely the origin of the magician's "Hocus pocus." To uninitiated ears "Hoc est corpus" sounds much like "Hocus pocus."

Yet even nonsuperstitious people use words to get things done. So in that sense words do have power—not inherent magical power, of course, but power nonetheless, power that derives from social convention. Philosophers of language call this use of words "performative."

A man fleeing down a dark alley hears the shouted words: "Stop! Police!" If he knows what's good for him, he'll stop. Immediately! That's an example of performative speech at work.

Mother sees little Sarah reaching out for the hot pan on the stove and yells, "No! Don't touch!" Sarah jerks her hand back. Mother has used performative speech, and Sarah has avoided getting scalded by boiling water.

The label on a bottle of medicine instructs: "Take one pill three times a day after meals." That's not informative speech, even though at first it may seem as though it is indeed sharing information. No, those are directions—another instance of performative language.

You're seated at the dinner table with guests, and in a courteous tone you say, "Sandra, would you please pass the salt?" Is that really a question you're asking? Are you asking for information about your guest's willingness to pass the saltshaker? No, you're using performative discourse. Your "question" was merely a polite way of making a demand of someone else. It's a command camouflaged as a question.

Standing in front of the entire congregation, you gaze fondly into the eyes of your sweetheart. Love glistens in both pairs of eyes as alternately both of you exchange wedding vows and say "I do." It is performative discourse when you pledge yourself to love, cherish, and remain faithful to your beloved.

"Do you swear to tell the truth, the whole truth, and nothing but the truth—so help you God?"

"I do," the witness vows, uttering performative words.

Standing in the kitchen about to make carrot cake, you pull a recipe card from the small file box and read the directions: "Sift . . . Add . . . Sprinkle . . . Stir . . . Pour . . . Spread . . . Bake . . ." Recipes are examples of performative speech.

The drill sergeant barks orders to his troops. "Forward march! . . . Right face! . . . About-face! . . . At ease!" And guess what. The soldiers in training march, turn, and stop. Why? Because the drill sergeant's words offer yet another example of performative communication.

Performative speech uses words to get something done. It precipitates behavior. Because words can thus be instrumental in causing something to happen, we sometimes call this type of communication *instrumental speech*, but it's the same thing as performative language.

Biblical Examples of Performative Discourse

The Bible contains numerous examples of performative speech.

In my opinion Genesis 1 offers the quintessential example of performative discourse. It tells us that God spoke Planet Earth into existence. "Let there be light. . . . Let there be a firmament. . . . Let the waters under the heaven be gathered together unto one place. . . . Let the earth bring forth grass. . . . Let there be lights in the . . . heaven. . . . Let the waters bring forth abundantly the moving creature that hath life. . . . Let the earth bring forth the living creature. . . . Let us make man in our image" (Gen. 1:3-26). The psalmist wrote: "He spake, and it was done; he commanded, and it stood fast" (Ps. 33:9). It is an example of performative speech embedded in cognitive discourse—God was uttering performative speech, and the biblical author of Genesis was using cognitive discourse, as discussed in the previous chapter.

When God delivered the Ten Commandments from Mount Sinai, He was using performative discourse. That's what commands and statutes are. When God uttered the Decalogue, He expected that obedience to each commandment would follow. And the Israelites gathered about the base of the mountain pledged, "All that the Lord hath said will we do, and be obedient" (Ex. 24:7). The laws of Scripture were calculated to elicit proper behavior from God's people, and their response was another occurrence of performative language.

Sometimes, of course, performative language does not produce the desired—and expected—response. The language may not then be effective, but it is nonetheless valid. Performative discourse does not violate human free will.

Nevertheless, when an Israelite made a vow, God expected him to perform it. "If a man vow a vow unto the Lord, or swear an oath to bind his soul with a bond; he shall not break his word, he shall do according to all that proceedeth out of his mouth" (Num. 30:2). "When thou vowest a vow unto God, defer not to pay it; for he hath no pleasure in fools: pay that which thou hast vowed. Better is it that thou shouldest not vow, than that shouldest vow and not pay" (Eccl. 5:4, 5).

Making a vow was serious business. To do so and then to ignore it meant that one's words uttered as a vow were lazy, idle words. They did not produce the action that the person had promised to perform, something inexcusable. The person making the vow had uttered performative words that produced no effect. It's like the son in Jesus' parable who promised his father that he would work in the garden and then did not. He made a promise that he never kept. Broken promises are idle words. So when Jesus said in Matthew 12:36 that God would hold us accountable for every idle word we speak, He was most likely not referring to puns, silly jokes, or expletives. Rather Jesus had in mind performative language that produces no performance.

Prophetic speech was often performative.

First, the prophets addressed the moral and spiritual life of the nation, calling into judgment the lapses in behavior of God's people. Joel cried out in the Lord's behalf, "Turn ye even to me with all your heart, and with fasting, and with weeping, and with mourning: and rend your heart, and not your garments, and turn unto the Lord your God" (2:12, 13).

Ezekiel pleaded: "Repent, and turn yourselves from all your transgressions; so iniquity shall not be your ruin. Cast away from you all your transgressions" (18:30, 31).

Such calls for repentance permeate the entire prophetic section of the Bible. And they all exemplify performative communication. Such calls to repentance were expected to produce . . . you guessed it, repentance!

Second, the prophets in God's name occasionally uttered predictions—predictions that more likely than not came to pass. Biblical predictions are another example of performative discourse, because the predictions were closely tied to the fulfillment. Utter the word, and the event would follow.

God through Isaiah said that just as the rain irrigates the earth, "so shall my word be that goeth forth out my mouth: it shall not return unto me void, but it shall accomplish that which I please, and it shall prosper in the thing whereto I sent it" (Isa. 55:11). "I am God, and there is none else; I am God, and there is none like me, declaring the end from the beginning, and from ancient times the things that are not yet done, saying, My counsel shall stand, and I will do all my pleasure: . . . yea, I have spoken it, I will also bring it to pass; I have purposed it, I will also do it" (Isa. 46:9-11).

Offering blessings in the Bible was a form of performative discourse. State the blessing, and the intended boon was expected to inexorably follow. That's why Esau was so upset when he learned that Isaac had uttered a blessing over the deceitful Jacob. To our way of thinking, Esau surely was overreacting when he wept and pleaded with his father like a little child. All those good things would come to pass—for Jacob and not for Esau, whom Isaac thought he was blessing.

"And Esau said unto his father, Hast thou but one blessing, my father? bless me, even me also, O my father" (Gen. 27:38).

Frantically Isaac searched his mind for a few words of blessing. What could he say? What kind of blessing could he yet come up with for heart-broken Esau, his favorite of the twins? Finally the old father "answered and said unto him, Behold, thy dwelling shall be the fatness of the earth, and of the dew of heaven from above; and by thy sword shalt thou live, and shalt serve thy brother; and it shall come to pass when thou shalt have the dominion, that thou shalt break his yoke from off thy neck" (verses 39, 40). It wasn't much of a blessing. Indeed, to Esau's ears it sounded more like a curse than a blessing—he would have to serve Jacob! No wonder Scripture adds: "And Esau hated Jacob because of the blessing wherewith his father blessed him" (verse 41).

Similarly, the ancients regarded cursings—the opposite side of the coin from blessings—also as performative speech. Curse someone or something, and the anticipated result was expected to follow. To curse someone was serious business and ideally done only in extenuating circumstances. The early chapters of Genesis speak of God's cursing the serpent and the earth in Eden (Gen. 3:14, 17).

After the Flood had ended and Noah had gotten himself drunk, his son Ham shamed his father by telling his brothers about their dad's nakedness rather than throwing a covering over Noah, as Shem and Japheth did as soon as they learned of his condition. Following that episode, when Noah was once again stone sober, he uttered a curse, saying, "Cursed be Canaan; a servant of servants shall he be unto his brethren" (Gen. 9:25). It was an omen of the later hostility between the Israelites and the Canaanites—an enmity believed to have been put into effect by Noah himself when he proclaimed that curse.

In fact, even the idea of cursing was so awesome that sometimes people would not even utter the Hebrew word for "curse." When Job had endured all those agonizing losses of property and children, even himself contracting a loathsome skin disease, his wife said to him, "Curse God, and die" (Job 2:9). At least that's how the KJV renders it. The fact is, though, that what she really said was "Bless God, and die." However, the KJV rendering of the Hebrew text is faithful to her intent. It was just that she didn't want to utter the word "curse," so she used its opposite as a euphemism or circumlocution for what she really intended to say!

In a culture that regarded blessings and cursings as performative language, it was a solemn matter to utter either. But the biblical world viewed cursing to be an especially serious—something one should not do in an offhanded or lighthearted manner. At times they considered it legitimate to curse someone, but a person must not do it casually as, say, in a pique of irritation.

Factuality is an issue when using informative discourse. *Rationality* is an issue when employing cognitive discourse. But factuality and rationality are not the issues with performative speech. *Validity—effectiveness*—is the key issue when we are dealing with the latter type of discourse.

CHAPTER 10

Kinds of Communication— Affective Discourse

My dad used to tell a story about an ardent beau who penned a note to his girlfriend. "For you—I'd climb the highest mountain. For your love—I'd swim the widest ocean. For one of your kisses—I'd trek the hottest desert. For one of your hugs—I'd walk through fire. PS: See you Sunday night if it doesn't rain." Exactly what was going on in that love note?

Affective Language

Affective discourse, that's what. No, the word isn't spelled incorrectly. We're talking not about *e*ffective language but about *a*ffective speech. When you see the word "affective," think of its sister "affection." The word "affective" was coined in 1623, so it's hardly a newcomer, but many of us are not used to seeing the word, even though psychologists use the term all the time. The word "affective" means "arising from or influencing feelings or emotions" (*Merriam-Webster's Collegiate Dictionary*, 11th edition).

Frequently affective speech resorts to hyperbole—often in somewhat outlandish terms and many times with a poetic form. Overstatement helps us to communicate our deepest feelings—emotions so profound, so moving, that we have difficulty expressing them. So we indicate their personal depth by resorting to extravagant words. And sober, sane people are savvy enough not to take literally such expressions of eloquence.

Affective discourse relies heavily on figurative language—metaphors, similes, etc. Connotation more than denotation is what one must look for in affective communication. You see, the face value of the words employed is not necessarily what the speaker intends. We need to look between the lines, so to speak, or beneath the surface, because what is said and what is meant are not always congruent. Affective language comes from the heart, not the brain. Sometimes affective language will be a story just for the story's sake. Most often affective language seeks to express one's feelings, but sometimes it might be used to rouse emotions in the recipient(s).

Poetry, including the lyrics for gospel songs and hymns, is a form of affective speech. The verses inside the birthday, anniversary, Christmas, get-well, and sympathy cards you send are still other examples of affective discourse. When a lover whispers, "I could never love anyone but you," to his sweetheart, he is using affective communication.

Back to my dad's silly anecdote. People inevitably chuckle at the incongruity of the young swain's message. Certainly this Don Juan was fickle—or was he? It's hard to tell—actually, impossible to know—from his little note. The humor arises because his starstruck love juxtaposed two different kinds of discourse in the one note.

The postscript was basically performative speech. The young man was committing himself to a certain course of action given the proper conditions. Perhaps he had to walk several miles to his sweetheart's home. Maybe he had to pedal a bike. Then again, it's possible that he had certain responsibilities that he had to fulfill in times of rain. Perhaps the weather bureau had forecast a hurricane. There may also be a touch of informative speech in the PS (yes, it's possible to blend several forms of discourse in a single communication), but I doubt it. The author didn't really want to share information. Probably his woman friend knew that rain had an effect on his ability to show up. I suspect that the postscript was performative language.

The incongruity—even humor—results because the author had appended a performative PS to the body copy of the note, which expressed his deep emotions of love and ardor. In short, the body of the note was affective communication. Some linguists refer to affective language as *expressive* communication. Whether one talks about either affective or expressive discourse, he or she is referring to the same thing.

Secular Examples of Affective Discourse

Sometimes affective discourse consists of only a single word, and occasionally it's almost nonsensical sounding. I bump my head on a low overhang and exclaim, "Ouch!" Disgusted because I can't make the plumbing under the sink fit properly, I retort, "Phooey!" On their own, such words don't make much sense. But uttered in specific circumstances, bystanders grasp their meaning. And sometimes we say them when no one is around, because expressing our strong feelings is all that matters to us at the moment.

The very emotional power of affective language can sometimes make us uncomfortable. The movie producers in Hollywood a generation ago wrestled with one word that Rhett Butler was supposed to say in *Gone With the Wind*. According to the book the film was based on, he says, "Frankly, my dear, I don't give a damn!" The movie moguls had to decide whether or not the word "damn" was profanity and unacceptable in a motion picture.

After consulting with linguists (yes, they took the matter very seriously), the producers decided that the word was *not* profanity and could flow from Rhett Butler's lips in the film. It was a watershed decision. Nowadays we hear the word and others far more profane and vulgar used regularly—even on family television programs.

What about such expressions? Is it wrong to use them? I suppose that it all depends on what one means by "wrong." Something may be wrong socially—serving meals in the bathroom or spitting on the living room floor—yet not be wrong morally.

Every culture has taboos. Some things are taboo because of fear or even because of awe. Other things become forbidden because of our sensitivity to certain issues. Certain things are so unpleasant to think about that we avoid bringing up those topics in conversation. And society proscribes other things because it considers them questionable or dirty, and so it would be a sign of impropriety to mention them publicly.

Taboos, however, are not eternal. Sooner or later they become modified for various reasons (some "good" and some "bad"), and ultimately what society one considered verboten becomes acceptable—even in polite company. Victorian men would not discuss or refer to a woman's legs in public. Today many would consider such a practice prudish. The object of the taboo might have no power in itself that we could consider forbidden. Rather people avoid discussing or referring to it for cultural and sociological reasons.

The producers of *Gone With the Wind* finally decided that the word "damn" had lost its overtones of theological damnation and implacable anger. They allowed the Rhett Butler to repeat the character's line from the novel.

We all use affective speech to express emotion. The issue involves how expressive we will allow ourselves to get. Most would croon "Mmmmmm!" when we taste something delicious, or "Ahhhh!" when something feels good. People will think nothing of shrieking "Eeeek!" when scared or muttering "Ouch!" hurt. It is basically a matter of *when* and *where* to call a halt to affective vocabulary—not *if*. Above all, it must be approached with great sensitivity. The Scriptures show many examples of acceptable affective speech.

Biblical Examples of Affective Discourse

Affective discourse is the language of adoration, of love, of awe, of worship. That's right, in worship—whether at home or in church, whether in song or in prayer—we utter affective speech. Sometimes we express the language of worship in single words: *Glory! Hallelujah! Amen! Hosanna!* Other times the language of worship can become downright verbose. "Praise ye the Lord. Praise God in his sanctuary: praise him in the firmament of his power. Praise him for his mighty acts: praise him according to his excellent greatness. Praise him with the sound of the trumpet: praise him with the psaltery and harp. Praise him with the timbrel and dance: praise him with stringed instruments and organs. Praise him upon the loud cymbals: praise him upon the high sounding cymbals. Let every thing that hath breath praise the Lord. Praise ye the Lord" (Ps. 150). And sometimes the language of rapture breaks forth into ecstatic language— tongues, we call it "glossolalia."

I used to refrain from singing the line "And clouds arise, and tempests blow, by order from Thy throne" in the well-known hymn "I Sing the Mighty Power of God." Those words really bothered me. I felt that they expressed bad theology. They sounded to me like Baal worship! After all, the Canaanite god Baal rode on the clouds and was the god of rain and storms.

Furthermore, I don't really believe that the God of heaven— YHWH—orders tempests. Consider the terrible record-breaking hurricanes that in recent years have wreaked havoc in Florida, Louisiana, and other states in the Deep South. If those hurricanes came by order from God's throne, then He acted most irresponsibly. Remember all the damage and huge monetary loss? Those storms destroyed life and produced great emotional trauma. Did God cause all that? I hope not. If He's in charge of the weather—as Baal was alleged to be—then He should be fired. Surely God can do better than that!

Then I learned the differences between informative, cognitive, performative, and affective discourse. And I came to realize that I had been causing a tempest in a teapot! Gospel songs use affective language—not cognitive or informative speech. The words convey emotion—not theology. I had been trying to make affective language do something that it wasn't intended to do. One must not construct theology from affective utterances. I learned that I should not take literally the language of worship.

You can see by now that affective language runs all through Scripture. Isaiah says, "In the Lord Jehovah is everlasting strength" (Isa. 26:4). And Job exclaims, "I know that thou canst do every thing" (Job 42:2). From these and other scriptural passages that sing of God's unfathomable power, we've theologized that God is omnipotent—all-powerful. Yet careful theologians warn us against going to extremes here. God cannot do that which is not an object of power. He cannot make square circles. Nor can He create a rock so big that He cannot move it. That the Lord cannot do that which is illogical or self-contradictory is something that most theologians agree upon.

In Hebrews 4:13 we read that "neither is there any creature that is not manifest in his sight: but all things are naked and opened unto the eyes of him with whom we have to do." From this verse and others like it, we have drawn the theological conclusion that God is omniscient—all-knowing.

Yet logic tells us that God really does not know absolutely everything. He cannot know our sins when He says that He will cast them into the depths of the sea and forget them (Micah 7:19). Nor can He know that which is not an object of knowledge—for example, that $2 + 3 = 10$.

These and other similar statements of awe, respect, adoration, and worship are affective utterances. We make a mistake when we take them literally and theologize from them—just as we would be wrong to take literally the expression "He's got the whole world in His hands," as Dr. John Harvey Kellogg did.

The sharing of emotions (or the evocation of emotions) is what counts most in affective discourse—not the sharing of information or the expression of abstract ideas. And so the issue in affective speech is not factuality (as in informative discourse) and not rationality (as in cognitive discourse) and not validity (as in performative discourse). *Sincerity*—unadulterated sharing of feelings—is what is at stake in affective discourse.

When a new mother turns to you and says, "Isn't my baby beautiful?" she's not asking for your ideas about beauty. Nor does she want information about esthetics. She's not even asking for your honest assessment of her infant's facial features. Instead, she's expressing her deep emotions of love and joy. And you should respond without hesitation, "Oh, isn't he darling!" even though you may really think that the child is just plain ugly. It would be cruel for you to share your honest opinion, and it's not dishonest for you to agree with the mother. In her use of affective speech she's seeking reaffirmation of her feelings, not impartial intellectual data.

Sometimes affective language masquerades as another form of speech—especially to the uninitiated or the unsuspecting. Surface appearances may lead you to assume that you're dealing with an example of informative discourse or cognitive speech. "The righteous cry, and the Lord heareth, and delivereth them out of all their troubles. . . . Many are the afflictions of the righteous: but the Lord delivereth him out of them all" (Ps. 34:17-19). At first glance you may think that you have here a clear case of informative speech—maybe even an example of performative discourse, if you decide that the passage is an oblique promise.

But start asking a few questions. Does God deliver good people out of *all* troubles? Read the next verse—about the righteous man: "He keepeth all his bones: not one of them is broken." Do Christians never break their bones? Do only the bad people suffer shattered arms or legs or broken hips?

And what about these verses? "They shall bear thee up in *their* hands, lest thou dash thy foot against a stone" (Ps. 91:12). "He will not suffer thy foot to be moved" (Ps. 121:3). "Then shalt thou walk in thy way safely, and thy foot shall not stumble" (Prov. 3:23). Do good people never stub their toe, never trip, never stumble and fall?

What at first glance appears to be informative or performative utterances turns out to be affective speech. The psalmist is extolling God's sustaining power, for which we can all be thankful, but we shouldn't understand the words as literally applying to every situation.

What about this example? "Bless the Lord, O my soul: and all that is within me, bless his holy name. Bless the Lord, O my soul, and forget not all his benefits" (Ps. 103:1, 2). Be careful, now! What kind of utterance is this? Do you think that it's a command—performative speech? Is the psalmist ordering himself to praise God? Not really. It is another example of affective speech, but dressed up like performative language—a commandment. Really an expression of emotion, it's an outburst of joyful enthusiasm, a paean of praise.

Jesus' words on the cross, "My God, my God, why hast thou forsaken me" (Matt. 27:46), provide us with another example of affective discourse. And His dying words to His mother, "Woman, behold thy son! . . . Behold thy mother!" (John 19:26, 27), fall into the same category, although they also have performative overtones to them. Christian tradition has it that John became a surrogate son to Mary, caring for her until she died.

Incidentally, compliments are also a form of affective discourse—if they are sincere—and should be so interpreted. Don't take them literally, as some people do. "That was a wonderful sermon, Pastor!" If a preacher took all such compliments at face value, he'd soon suffer from an overinflated ego! Compliments may be well-meaning—and here sincerity is the virtue—but they are not informative speech and so are not factually true. (And if you haven't yet figured it out, the Song of Solomon consists of affective language. Read it that way and not the way one woman I knew interpreted it—as predictive prophecy.)

Affective communication is a legitimate use of language. We meet it every day, but we must recognize it for what it is—even when it is in the Bible. Otherwise we shall live in a world of delusions.

CHAPTER 11

Kinds of Communication— Phatic Discourse

Good morning! How are you today, Mrs. Hogart?" The church greeter stretches his lips taut in a forced smile and reaches to shake her hand.

"Eh?" the elderly parishioner responds as she cups her hand behind her good ear.

"I said, 'How are you today, Mrs. Hogart?'"

"Not too good, sonny," she replies in a not-too-soft-but-tremulous voice. "My corns are killing me. My postnasal drip won't quit. At breakfast a raspberry seed got caught under my dentures. I'm having bad gas pains. My bowels haven't moved for days, and my hemorrhoids itch and burn like you wouldn't believe."

A puzzled expression by now has replaced the smile on Bob Drake's face as Mrs. Hogart shuffles off into the church sanctuary. Yet why should the greeter be perplexed? Hadn't he gotten exactly what he'd asked for? Hadn't he inquired, "How are you?" of Mrs. Hogart?

The truth is that the greeter had repeated that salutation twoscore, threescore, and maybe more times that morning. And not once had he expected people to respond with a list of their aches and pains. That's why crotchety Mrs. Hogart's list of complaints startled him so.

How many times each day does someone in America repeat those three words: "How are you?" And almost every time, the speaker never intends to elicit a litany of physical ailments. We don't seek a status report of physical well-being when we mouth that greeting—unless, of course, we are a physician trying to diagnose a patient's problem.

What kind of talk is this? When we say "How are you?" it's barely a question. We aren't seeking information, sharing ideology, or barking a command. Nor are we even expressing a deep feeling. In fact, we don't even literally mean what we have said. That's why Mrs. Hogart's "organ recital" surprised the greeter at church. She took his words literally, but Mr. Drake didn't mean them literally. He expected her to parrot, "Fine, thank you," even though her gallbladder was acting up. Even a terse "Not so good, thanks" raises our eyebrows!

It's truly a strange use of language—to ask a question when we seek absolutely no information. We repeat a clause that has no more meaning than an echo. Although we sound caring, we really couldn't care less. While we know what the three words mean, we really don't mean what we have said. And we go through this bizarre custom numerous times each day—thousands upon thousands of times during a lifetime!

The word "phatic" first came into use in 1922. Derived from a Greek word (*phatos*) meaning "spoken," it denotes "speech used for social . . . purposes rather than for communicating information" (*Merriam-Webster's Collegiate Dictionary*, 11th edition). Sometimes experts call it cohesive language.

We've been talking about phatic utterances. Polish-born Bronislaw Malinowski, considered to be one of the most important anthropologists of the twentieth century, originated the name to describe speech that does not convey emotion, as does affective communication, though phatic speech tends to convey a general feeling of casual friendliness. Basically, phatic discourse establishes an air of sociability. Period.

Phatic discourse is generally not extensive and is usually stereotypical and formulaic. Expressing friendliness and safety, it deals with superficial interpersonal relationships. Don't let that word "superficial" act as a red herring, however. We're not talking about something bad.

Secular Examples of Phatic Discourse

All of us resort to phatic speech throughout the day. The phone rings, and we answer, "Hello." We begin correspondence with "Dear Mr. Jones." (Is Mr. Jones really a dear? He may be somebody's dear, but is he *yours*?) And we end the letter with "Sincerely yours" or "Yours truly" or in the case of close friends and relatives, "Love." Shaking the hand of a total stranger, we say, "Nice to meet you." (What's so nice about it? You haven't even gotten acquainted with the person yet.) When a conversation ends, we announce, "Goodbye." ("Goodbye" is an elided form of "God be with ye." Can an atheist say "goodbye" and be sincere about it?) Perhaps we introduce a friend to someone else with "I'd like you to meet Susie Ethelwaite." (Why are we so eager to have someone else become acquainted with her?) Perhaps we conclude another conversation with "Thank you so much." (How much is "so much"? And how *really* thankful are you?) Encountering a salesperson at the door or a telemarketer on the phone, we declare, "Sorry. I don't want any." (Do we really get emotionally regretful?) As guests depart we shout, "Come again." (Are we *sure* we want them to return?) "Hey, good buddy," the trucker belches into the CB microphone, and later, "10-4, good buddy." (Has he even met the CBer at the other end?) "Great weather," we say as we grin at a stranger. (How do you know that the other person cares about the kind of weather we're experiencing? And do they really think it's "great"?)

Although such language has no real content to it, phatic communication does provide a certain sense of solidarity among people. You're riding alone in an elevator and heading for the tenth floor. It stops at the third floor, and a big, brusque-looking brute of a man steps in—glaring tattoos on his arms. The door slides shut, locking just the two of you inside together—in that tiny enclosure. Pressing back into the corner, you try to appear nonchalant. The big bruiser turns around, smiles slightly, and says, "Hi! Beautiful day, huh?"

The tenseness flows from your body. The (apparent) threat is over. "Yeah," you reply weakly and manage a smile in return.

Phatic language conveys little—if any—information. It promises nothing. The words themselves are practically devoid of meaning (denotation). And even emotional overtones (connotation) are almost nonexistent. Nevertheless, the expressions—mechanical though they may be—do offer a vague sense that makes people feel a bit more comfortable with one another. Such communication helps establish rapport with others. When we resort to phatic utterances, we're creating a "warm fuzzy."

Other examples of phatic speech include: "See ya!" "Gesundheit!" "God bless you!" "Never seen it so cold!" "Best of everything!" "Best wishes." "There, there!" "Now, now. It's OK." "Everything's going to be all right." "Come, come!" You can probably think of many more.

What about jocular comments? Are they a separate kind of speech—in a category all of their own? Most likely not. If used as an icebreaker at the beginning of a speech, they constitute phatic communication. But if said simply to make people laugh and have a good time, then they're examples of affective discourse.

Biblical Examples of Phatic Discourse

People in the ancient Near East also used phatic speech, although they certainly didn't know the name that Malinowski gave to it so many millennia later. However, we do not find a lot of examples of it in Scripture. *Shalom* served as the standard Hebrew greeting—"Peace!" The Greeks often used the term *chairein*—"Greetings." The Romans typically said *Ave*—"Hail!"

In the Old Testament book of Proverbs we find an expression used again and again and again: "My son, . . ." (1:8, 10, 15; 2:1; 3:1, 11, 21; 4:10, 20; 5:1, 20; 6:1, 3, 20; etc.). We should not take this as informative language indicating that a specific biological father speaking to his biological male offspring. Rather, we should understand it as phatic speech. The sage giving the proverbial advice is addressing in a friendly and kindly manner any young man. It is the equivalent of "to whom it may concern," but with a more engaging overtone.

Another expression we find in Scripture is "Fear not . . ." (Gen. 15:1; 21:17; 26:24; 35:17; 43:23; 50:19; Ex. 14:13; 20:20; Joshua 8:1; 10:25; Judges 4:18; 6:23; Ruth 3:11; 1 Sam. 4:20; 12:20; 2 Sam. 9:7; 13:28; Isa. 7:4; Jer. 46:28; Dan. 10:12; Joel 2:21; Mal. 3:5; Matt. 1:20; 10:31; Luke 2:10; Rev. 1:17; etc.). One might construe it as affective language intended to produce an emotional response in the part of the recipient of the words, and in some cases that might indeed be correct. However, in many cases it seems to me that because of its frequent use it has become another example of phatic speech.

The apostle Paul habitually opened and/or closed his Epistles with certain stereotyped formulaic expressions. "*Grace* to you, and *peace,* from God our Father and the Lord Jesus Christ" (Philemon 3; cf. 2 Thess. 1:2). "The *grace* of the Lord Jesus Christ be with your spirit" (Philemon 25). "*Grace, mercy,* and *peace,* from God the Father and the Lord Jesus Christ our Saviour" (Titus 1:4). "*Grace* be with you all" (Titus 3:15). "*Grace, mercy,* and *peace* from God our Father and Jesus Christ our Lord" (1 Tim. 1:2; cf. 2 Tim. 1:2). "*Grace* be with thee" (1 Tim. 6:21; cf. 2 Tim. 4:22). "*Grace* to you and *peace*" (1 Thess. 1:1). "The *grace* of our Lord Jesus Christ be with you all" (2 Thess. 3:18; cf. 1 Thess. 5:28). We could multiply the examples.

Paul in his epistolary salutations blended the Hebrew phatic salutation *shalom* (peace) with a pun on the Greek phatic greeting *chairein—charis* (grace). Both *shalom* and *chairein* were phatic terminology that he adapted and used for beginning and ending his letters—just as we start our letters with "dear" and conclude them with "sincerely."

But Paul's usage was phatic speech with a twist. He modified the phatic terminology so that it conformed to his Christian theology, which emphasized both peace and grace. So there were overtones, perhaps, in Paul's salutations of cognitive language, but I feel that we should not try to extract from his usage very much theological milk.

We find another example of phatic discourse in 3 John. "Beloved, I wish above all things that thou mayest prosper and be in health" (1:2). John began his letter with this greeting—much the same way as we often open a letter with a similar wish: "I hope that this letter finds you in good health" or something to that effect. It seems to me that we press this phatic expression too far when we use it to tell people that God's inspired apostle was here echoing His wish for them—good health. I would assume that God surely does want us to enjoy good health, but I don't think that 3 John 1:2 is a good proof text for that concept. In my view, it is a purely phatic utterance and not an example of cognitive discourse.

Interestingly, Jesus told His disciples not to use phatic speech on their missionary journeys. "Salute no man by the way" (Luke 10:4). Jesus was not here forbidding a private first class from saluting a drill sergeant, and we shouldn't use His instruction in that way. Rather, He was talking about the exchange of greetings. It's not that He wanted Christians to snub others. If you pass me by and refuse to say "Hello," I'm going to think that you're stuck-up—or perhaps angry with me. Is that what Jesus intended?

I doubt it. In the ancient Near East people had elaborate greeting routines—as many in the Far East still have. To greet someone along the road could mean that you would have to go through a complex exchange of phatic language. To do this had the potential for delaying the disciples—maybe for as much as half a day. Jesus had sent them on urgent business, and they were not to greet just anyone along the way. Time was too precious. G. B. Caird points out that "the Oriental has never been sparing with his greetings" (*The Language and Imagery of the Bible*, p. 33).

If, for instance, you were to compliment a Chinese father on the beauty of his daughter, he would probably tell you that she is ugly, denying your compliment. Bruce Malina attributes such a reaction as a response to having one's honor affronted. Dyadic personalities, Malina affirms, regard compliments as a form of aggression (*The New Testament World*, p. 79). Compliments constitute a kind of negative challenge that must be repudiated if one wishes to save face. (Yes, compliments are another instance of phatic speech.)

Jesus responded to one compliment in a way that has perplexed Western readers of the Gospels. A ruler approached Him and uttered the complimentary greeting (phatic discourse), "*Good Master*, what shall I do to inherit eternal life?" (Luke 18:18). From *our* perspective we would expect that Jesus would have basked in such a compliment. We would expect that He would have glowed with pleasure that here was someone who appreciated His moral perfection of character! Also we would think that He should have instantly focused on the man's question and pointed out the way of salvation. After all, the ruler did ask *the* question of all questions! Can you think of a more important question to ask of anyone—especially of Jesus?

But Jesus didn't respond as we would. Instead of thanking the man for his complimentary words, Jesus acted offended. "Why callest thou me good? none is good, save one, that is, God" (verse 19).

Here was a seeker after truth, but Jesus initially engaged him in phatic discourse. Only later did He address the religious and spiritual issue. Jesus played the phatic game (along with the challenge and riposte game) first. Not until afterward did He concentrate on the religious issue.

Sometimes we Westerners suggest that Jesus wanted to make a theological point in His response to the ruler's compliment. But Jesus was not engaging in either cognitive or informative discourse. He was employing phatic speech. We look in vain for theological content and misconstrue what was happening if we do so. Phatic words are not spiritual apples from which we can press theological cider!

Jesus used phatic discourse when He prefaced some of His teachings with "Verily, verily, I say . . . " Such words helped produce psychological bonding with His audience. It was rather like what happens when the Navy ensign shouts over the intercom, "Now hear this, now hear this . . ." or when you wag your finger in someone's face and say, "Believe you me . . ."

Despite its lack of concrete data, phatic speech is a legitimate use of language. Christians need not avoid it as if it were a form of the "idle words" that Jesus condemned (Matt. 12:36). Even though He commanded His disciples to refrain from getting bogged down in elaborate exchanges of phatic communion while on their missionary journeys, He Himself employed it, as did His disciples. Christians need not eschew a moderate use of phatic expressions.

CHAPTER 12

Kinds of Communication— The Quiz

Let's assume for the moment that you found the previous chapters on communication helpful. I hope that you'd like to put this information to use when you study the Bible. However, it isn't always easy to sort out the five different types of discourse. At times we may disagree as to what sort of language the biblical writer is employing in a given instance—informative, cognitive, performative, affective, or phatic. Just how can a person decide which type of discourse a specific passage of Scripture is? I have no easy answer to that question other than it can require careful thought and analysis.

Let's try something, though. Why not take the following test? See if you agree with my answers. The first few questions will deal with secular communication, but the final examples will come from the Bible. Check the box (or boxes) that you think identifies the kind of language that each is an example of.

1. "Goodbye."
  ❑ Informative   ❑ Cognitive   ❑ Performative
  ❑ Affective   ❑ Phatic

2. "You're the best husband/wife ever!"
  ❑ Informative   ❑ Cognitive   ❑ Performative
  ❑ Affective   ❑ Phatic

3. **"God doesn't make junk." (Said of a person with a disability.)**
   - ❏ Informative
   - ❏ Cognitive
   - ❏ Performative
   - ❏ Affective
   - ❏ Phatic

4. **"There they crucified him" (Luke 23:33).**
   - ❏ Informative
   - ❏ Cognitive
   - ❏ Performative
   - ❏ Affective
   - ❏ Phatic

5. **"The Lord our God is one Lord" (Deut. 6:4).**
   - ❏ Informative
   - ❏ Cognitive
   - ❏ Performative
   - ❏ Affective
   - ❏ Phatic

6. **"Give unto the Lord glory and strength" (Ps. 29:1).**
   - ❏ Informative
   - ❏ Cognitive
   - ❏ Performative
   - ❏ Affective
   - ❏ Phatic

7. **"The Lord gave Jehoiakim into [Nebuchadnezzar's] hand" (Dan. 1:2).**
   - ❏ Informative
   - ❏ Cognitive
   - ❏ Performative
   - ❏ Affective
   - ❏ Phatic

8. **"My soul doth magnify the Lord" (Luke 1:46).**
   - ❏ Informative
   - ❏ Cognitive
   - ❏ Performative
   - ❏ Affective
   - ❏ Phatic

9. **"Thou hatest all evildoers" (Ps. 5:5, RSV).**
   - ❏ Informative
   - ❏ Cognitive
   - ❏ Performative
   - ❏ Affective
   - ❏ Phatic

10. **The Lord's "wrath is quickly kindled" (Ps. 2:11, RSV).**
    - ❏ Informative
    - ❏ Cognitive
    - ❏ Performative
    - ❏ Affective
    - ❏ Phatic

11. **"Thus saith the Lord to his anointed, to Cyrus" (Isa. 45:1).**
    - ❏ Informative
    - ❏ Cognitive
    - ❏ Performative
    - ❏ Affective
    - ❏ Phatic

12. **"Happy shall he be, that . . . dasheth thy little ones against the stones" (Ps. 137:9).**
    - ❏ Informative
    - ❏ Cognitive
    - ❏ Performative
    - ❏ Affective
    - ❏ Phatic

13. **"Peace be to you" (Gen. 43:23).**
    - ❏ Informative
    - ❏ Cognitive
    - ❏ Performative
    - ❏ Affective
    - ❏ Phatic

14. **"Be of good cheer; . . . be not afraid" (Matt. 14:27).**
    - ❏ Informative
    - ❏ Cognitive
    - ❏ Performative
    - ❏ Affective
    - ❏ Phatic

15. **"This do in remembrance of me" (Luke 22:19).**
    - ❏ Informative
    - ❏ Cognitive
    - ❏ Performative
    - ❏ Affective
    - ❏ Phatic

16. **"Blessed are the meek" (Matt. 5:5).**
    - ❏ Informative
    - ❏ Cognitive
    - ❏ Performative
    - ❏ Affective
    - ❏ Phatic

17. **"Against him came up Nebuchadnezzar king of Babylon" (2 Chron. 36:6).**
    - ❏ Informative
    - ❏ Cognitive
    - ❏ Performative
    - ❏ Affective
    - ❏ Phatic

18. **Jesus is man.**
    - ❏ Informative
    - ❏ Cognitive
    - ❏ Performative
    - ❏ Affective
    - ❏ Phatic

19. **Jesus is God.**
    - ❏ Informative
    - ❏ Cognitive
    - ❏ Performative
    - ❏ Affective
    - ❏ Phatic

Well, that's the test. Below is my answer key. How did you do on this quiz? Remember that we may not always see eye-to-eye. Because of that, I'm also adding some explanatory thoughts that will let you know why I have made the specific identification(s) that I did.

1. Phatic—As mentioned previously, the word "goodbye" was an combination of "God be with ye" when first used in 1580. Even atheists say "goodbye." Why? Are they compromising their anti-God philosophy? No. The root meaning of a word doesn't always carry through in use many years distant from when the word was coined. When we use words in phatic discourse, denotation has almost no role to play. Goodbye no longer has a theological denotation, so even atheists use the term.

2. Affective—When we voice our emotions, the literal meaning of the words should typically be overlooked. The spouse who says this has not taken a poll of all other spouses around the world, done a psychological profile of them, or given them a personality test. So for a wife to say to her husband, "You're the best husband in the whole world," she's not engaging in informative discourse. Rather, she's expressing her feelings of love and ardor. What counts is that she's maintaining a relationship by using the extravagant language of love.

3. Affective—At first glance this may appear to be an example of either informative or cognitive speech. But think about it for a moment. When you speak of God, you're not using informative speech, because you cannot empirically prove the existence of God even in theory. So whoever made this statement about a person with a disability wasn't saying something that he or she knew with strong warrant. Furthermore, the assertion states absolutely nothing about the origin of mental and/or physical disorders, therefore ruling out informative discourse. But what about cognitive communication? Do you really truly believe that God is responsible for people born with muscular dystrophy or cerebral palsy? Was it His fault that thalidomide babies were born without arms or without legs? Not the God I worship! So I don't think that this is an example of cognitive speech. It is, however, an example of affective speech—someone expressing the emotion of compassion and trying to elicit feelings of personal value in the "victim."

4. Informative—The Gospel writer is identifying the place Jesus was crucified. In fact, Luke names the site—Calvary. It is the kind of data that some contemporary of Jesus—or of Luke—could have found eyewitnesses who could have confirmed the name of the place Jesus died on the cross. Theoretically, this piece of information was capable of being independently verified. And one needn't contact a believer. Even a Roman soldier could have readily stated that yes, indeed, Jesus had been executed at the spot called Calvary (aka Golgotha).

5. Cognitive—This is the famous Shema that pious Jews repeat every day. At first glance it may sound as though it is an example of informative discourse, but it really isn't. This is a statement of faith, not of knowledge. How could any human being ever come up with empirical proof that (a) there is a God and that (b) this God is one?

6. Affective—Almost everything found in the Psalms—poetry—is an example of affective speech. It would be ridiculous to take this passage of Scripture literally. Can any human being actually add to God's strength or power? He's already omnipotent, right? How can we weak and puny creatures give strength to our all-powerful God? And how can we inglorious critters increase God's glory? No, this is not performative speech in the strictest sense, because we cannot literally do what the verse tells us to do. But it does make sense to view this passage as affective communication—an expression of one's awe of and love for God. He does not lack something that you and I could bestow upon Him.

7. Cognitive—Were you tempted to label this informative speech? That could be a hard temptation to resist. But how could anyone ever independently verify that the Hebrew God, YHWH, actively stood up for Nebuchadnezzar and enabled him to conquer the Hebrew people? What caused Nebuchadnezzar's victory over Jerusalem? Well, if he had more soldiers who were better trained than the Judahite army, one could state *that* as informative speech. But that's not what the text says. It is a statement of belief, of faith, and thus it is cognitive discourse.

8. Affective—Mary is ecstatic over the news that she will give birth to the long-awaited Messiah. In fact, she bursts into song here. Lyrics are an example of affective speech. Again, no one would want to take these words literally. How could a small and frail teenager magnify the infinite God? That would be nonsense, right? If that was really what Mary meant, you'd scold her, wouldn't you? You'd set her straight. Just because she'll be the mother of Jesus Christ gives her no right to become so arrogant that she would think she could enlarge God!

9. Affective—First, of course, this assertion comes from one of the psalms. So we aren't going to take it as either informative or cognitive communication. This is poetry. The psalmist is putting his deep emotional state into words. Besides, what kind of theology is this, anyway? Isn't it true that God loves everyone—including sinners? Isn't it theologically true that God loves sinners but hates their sins? However, that is *not* what the psalmist states here. This verse expresses appalling theology even though it is straight from the pages of the Bible, voiced by an inspired Bible writer!

10. Affective—Yes, there's a lot of affective speech in Scripture. If this were an example of cognitive communication, we'd have the same problem with this verse that we had with the previous passage. It's simply bad theology. Once again the psalmist is pouring out his emotions, but elsewhere Scripture declares that God is not quick to anger but is long-suffering (Neh. 9:17). Even Psalms 103 and 145 remind us that God is slow to get angry—a flat contradiction of Psalm 2:11, RSV.

11. Cognitive—This verse is quite amazing! God calls Cyrus, a pagan king, "my Messiah." Yes, that's what the Hebrew says. Don't jump to the conclusion that it is informative speech because the proper noun Cyrus appears in the text. When we find passages of Scripture in which God speaks, we're most likely looking at cognitive discourse. We're beyond the realm of being able to verify empirically the data presented in the text. How can any of Isaiah's readers—and that includes you and me—independently prove what God says about anyone or anything? Not being privy to His thoughts, we simply can't. That Cyrus is God's Messiah is a matter of faith, not empirically verifiable knowledge. Cyrus was a good king, but was he *that* good? However, he did let the captive Jews return to their devastated homeland, and for that he merited the title of "anointed one" or "messiah." God is saying that He is using Cyrus for a divine purpose—to return the prisoners of war to Jerusalem.

12. Affective—What a verse! Here we have vindictiveness at its most venomous. The Bible has many beatitudes. This is one of them. But what a beatitude! Blessed or happy (in the sense of being fortunate) is the soldier who bashes an infant's brains out? Surely this is not informative or cognitive speech! It is another example of emotional outburst, and it doesn't surprise us that it appears in the Psalms. However, it is affective speech with strong overtones of performative language. (See comments on number 16 below.)

13. Phatic—Scripture uses this heartening greeting on several occasions. It's a way of reassuring someone who has every right to be unsettled by what is happening—perhaps the person is receiving some sort of epiphany or revelation from God. However, in this instance Joseph, the vizier of Egypt, says it to the very brothers who had sold him into slavery. They had every right to have been afraid of Joseph, who now had the civil power to turn the tables on them and imprison them all. In fact, he *did* imprison one of his brothers, Simeon. In Luke 24:36 Jesus said something similar to His frightened disciples as they cowered in the upper room after His resurrection. It was a standard Hebrew salutation.

14. Phatic—Jesus is here greeting His disciples as He is walking on the water. They think that He is a ghost. (Hadn't their mothers told them that there's no such thing as a ghost?) The intent of these few words is to set the disciples at ease—one of the most common uses of phatic discourse. If you regard this statement as a direct command (can we really make emotions obey?), then you might have chosen "performative" also.

15. Performative—Jesus is instituting the ongoing commemoration of His salvific death and resurrection—the Communion service. He tells the disciples to repeat this ritual in His memory. It's a command—an order, if you will—from Jesus. And by resorting to the imperative mood, He anticipates that the result will follow. The disciples *will do* exactly what He tells them.

16. Performative—Remember that generally blessings and cursings in biblical times were forms of performative speech. Macarisms, as scholars refer to these blessings, express one's wish for beneficence to fall upon others. Verbalizing the blessing unleashes power, and the desired result will follow. Many times such blessings carry overtones of affective discourse also. When people uttered a blessing, they were usually experiencing strong positive emotions.

17. Informative—You probably found this one easy, didn't you? It is a statement of fact, having the potential of being independently verified. In fact, we *do* have extrabiblical confirmation for it. Nebuchadnezzar prepared his own court chronicles that mentioned his attack on Judah: "Seventh year: In the month Kislimu, the king of Akkad [Nebuchadnezzar] . . . marched against Syria, encamped against the city of Judah and seized the town on the second day of the month Adar. He captured the king. . . . He took much booty from it and sent [it] to Babylon"

(Tablet ANE 21946 in the British Museum; see James B. Pritchard, *Ancient Near Eastern Texts,* pp. 563, 564).

18. Informative; 19. Cognitive—These last two are actually trick questions, and my identification of the types of discourse used will require a bit of explanation.

Let's quickly review the difference between informative and cognitive discourse.

Informative language, on the one hand, deals with data—that which we can empirically verify. The content is what we commonly call "knowledge." *Cognitive language,* on the other hand, deals with opinion and ideas—mental or theoretical constructs. Its content is what we commonly call "belief."

Notice the difference between the following two examples. *Informative language*—Cyrus, son of Cambyses, became king of Persia c. 558 B.C. and died in battle c. 530 B.C. This is a datum of knowledge. *Cognitive language*—Cyrus, king of Persia, was God's shepherd (Isa. 44:28) and Messiah (Isa. 45:1). Here we have a datum of belief.

Now we can turn to the sentences in items 18 and 19: "Jesus is man" and "Jesus is God." Grammatically, the two sentences are indistinguishable. Each consists of a proper noun (Jesus), a verb (is), and a predicate nominative (man; God). But we must not be fooled by the grammatical similarity. The grammatical structure of the two sentences may be identical, but each sentence represents a different kind of discourse. Let's look at each sentence separately so that you can see why I've differentiated between them.

"Jesus is man." We could just as easily have said, "Jesus is human." It would have meant the same thing, except that we substituted a predicate adjective (human) for the predicate nominative (man). As a result of personal experience and empirical research, we know how to classify and evaluate a member of *Homo sapiens.* We ourselves are human beings, and it takes one to know one! Thus we have no problem identifying women as human beings no matter whether they are tall or short, thin or fat, blond or brunet, Caucasian or Negroid. Likewise we have no problem identifying men as human beings even though they might be lanky or squatty, underweight or overweight, redheaded or bald, Asian or Negroid.

Yes, we *know* what constitutes a human being. We don't need a field guide to mammals to help us make the identification—even though humans come in various colors and sizes and shapes.

Additionally, we have learned from empirical evidence what is "normal" for human beings. Research has taught us how to measure blood pressure, temperature, and respiration—and what those values should be. Today we even have scientific methods that involve DNA analysis for identifying species—determining whether or not an entity is human, a member of *Homo sapiens*.

Now let's turn to Jesus of Nazareth. People walked and talked with Him. They saw, heard, smelled, and felt Him. His neighbors at Nazareth knew Him. Their children had played with Him when He was a child. It's an empirical datum that Jesus is man—human. No one—not even a skeptic—would deny this. That's why the sentence "Jesus is man" is an example of informative speech. It shares data—information—that theoretically we could independently and empirically substantiate. *This is a statement of **knowledge***. Anyone—Buddhist, Jew, Hindu, Muslim, or atheist—could agree with this assertion.

But **"Jesus is God"** is an entirely different type of sentence from the one that says "Jesus is man." Yes, really. Permit me to explain. We cannot detect God by our senses. None of us has seen or heard or felt or smelled Him. He remains outside our senses. "No man hath seen God at any time" (1 John 4:12). (This from John, who made the most definitive assertions about Jesus' being God!) That's why we cannot objectively prove God's existence. Fact is, we don't know how to classify and evaluate a member of Deity. "Human" as an adjective refers to a species, and "man" is a species. But is "God" a species? Is "God" a phylum? Is "God" a kingdom?

It would be preposterous for people who gazed upon Baby Jesus to have said, "Ohhh, what a cute baby God!" When Mary changed Jesus' diapers, she saw—and smelled—a human infant. There is no field guide to help us identify God. Empirically we have no way to measure divine blood pressure, temperature, and respiration. We have no scientific method of determining from DNA whether or not a living entity is divine.

Because we cannot even prove beyond a shadow of a doubt that God exists, it is not an empirical datum that Jesus is God—divine. "There's no lab test for Christ-ness" (*U.S. News & World Report*, July 24-31, 2000, p. 40).

That's why the sentence "Jesus is God" is an example of cognitive speech. It shares a theoretical construct that we cannot independently and empirically verify. *It is a statement of **belief—faith**.*

CHAPTER 13

Story Time—Introduction

W hen our granddaughter was 4 and 5 years old, she loved stories, especially when she was riding in the car. It didn't matter to little Kelli if they weren't all that dramatic. In fact, an extemporaneous made-up tale about some nonexistent character worked quite well. Or an account of what she had done so far that day equally amused her. Of course, her parents read books to her each day, including a Bible story for worship in the evening.

We're all a bit like Kelli, because we all like stories—even those of us who are many times Kelli's age. Jesus knew that, and the Gospel accounts of His ministry are punctuated with additional stories—parables, we call them. And the daily fare on television is more often than not a drama (another synonym for story): a soap opera, a rerun of an old Western, a sitcom, a dramatization about the life of some historical figure, a criminal investigation movie, an espionage thriller, a reenactment of a famous battle . . . You get the picture.

In keeping with our Western tastes, narratives share in common certain characteristics.

They have a backdrop or scene—maybe several—for the story, including both time and place. Each scene shows movement of some sort, including both progress and setbacks. Transitions tie the various scenes together.

A plot of some sort is a must—a series of actions, with some sort of conflict at the heart. The plot is the unfolding dramatic progression, and we feel most satisfied when we have some kind of resolution at the very end so that, for example, good triumphs over evil.

A story will often introduce several main characters. Usually we read about a protagonist (hero), who is usually the central character, and of an antagonist (villain), who is the nemesis (opponent) of the leading character. Both are essential. A good story doesn't have to tell you what each person is like. Instead, how that individual acts or doesn't act and what the person says or doesn't say can give perceptive readers insight into the character's personality. A good story doesn't *tell* you that Mary is kind—it *shows* you that she is thoughtful of others through her deeds and behavior.

Many stories trace the growth of the protagonist. A good narrative just doesn't sit there in neutral. Things happen—we call them events. Characters do things, and things get done to them. The characters' roles remain consistent throughout the story.

Conversation keeps the story line moving. And skillfully crafted dialogue helps make the actors come alive. What characters say should be in keeping with their personalities and roles. A hard-boiled streetwise gangster from New York City's Hell's Kitchen won't talk like a country gal from the American Deep South.

A good narrative blends suspense with emotion—emotion for both the actors and the readers. Sometimes the suspense is scary, but other times it's just sufficient to hold our interest. When the narrative ends, we feel a sense of resolution and completion.

The author tells each story from a specific viewpoint. Point of view can be either subjective or objective. The subjective viewpoint presents the story from inside the hero's mind. The objective viewpoint relates it from outside the hero's mind. Usually a well-crafted story doesn't change viewpoint but stays with either the subjective or objective perspective.

The subjective viewpoint is an insider's perspective and often told from a first-person position, though not always. The storyteller may write about his or her own personal experience, referring to himself or herself as "I" throughout. Or the author may write the story from the viewpoint of the hero. Once again the narrative employs the first-person voice, but here it's not the voice of the writer but that of the main character.

The objective viewpoint is an outsider's perspective and perhaps told with the third-person voice. "He" or "she" does the talking and acting within the narrative. Or the author may be telling someone else's story or has another person—maybe an unseen observer—relate the hero's experiences.

Basically, an author can write three kinds of stories. The *character story* focuses on the experiences of a person or group of people. A narrative about a personal experience is a character story. Biographies and autobiographies offer other examples. The *idea story* often explores a "what if" question. Problems get resolved in idea stories. The *theme story* dramatizes a truth that we can typically encapsulate in a single theme sentence.

Biblical Narrative Criticism

The Bible is jam-packed with stories, and many of the same markers of a good American story appear in those recorded in Scripture. However, ancient Near Eastern authors composed the scriptural accounts, and they didn't necessarily subscribe to the same canons of narration that Western authors do.

Nonetheless, astute readers of the stories found in God's Word will look for clues that can help them understand the dynamics inherent in them. Which character or characters do the talking in the story? Which character or characters say nothing? Which character or characters remain silent until the end of the story? What verbs does the author use? Who is the active person? Who is the passive one? What nouns appear? What modifiers get used? Are there hints of other biblical passages within the story itself? What literary structures shape the story? What genre, if any, is the story written in? In what place does the story begin? Does it end in the same place or in a different location? Who is the implied original audience for the story? Might there be an implied contemporary readership? Who is the narrator of the story? Is this person different from the traditional (biblical) author? What point of view lies behind the narrative? What symbolic language might the narrative employ?

Another factor worthy of considerable thought is the name of the characters and places in a story. Most biblical names had a special meaning, and if we understand that, it can give us insights into the narrative itself. For example, the proper nouns in the story of Samson are most often puns. We don't know the exact derivation of the name Samson, but it probably means "little sun"—or Sunny.

Timnath, a city, whose name is the Hebrew word for "portion," appears in a story in which the portion of 30 sheets and 30 changes of clothing ended up going to the wrong people. So Little Sun went to

Ashkelon—the name has something to do with weighing out money and goods—and there killed 30 people for their clothing.

Later Sunny was at Lehi, a town whose name meant "jawbone." There he killed 1,000 men with the jawbone of a donkey. Later Sunny journeyed to Gaza—the "fortress"—where during the night he walked away with the city's front gate on his back. Then he went to Sorek—the name means "bright-red, choice grapes." (Why a Nazirite was visiting the vineyards is anyone's guess.) While there he fell in love with Delilah, whose name has the connotation of "flirt" or "coquette."

Later David, before he took the throne, met up with a man by the name of Nabal, Hebrew for "fool." And, of course, Nabal played the fool, refusing to give David provisions, even though David's ragtag group of bandits had protected the wealthy landowner and his property. Abigail, Nabal's wife, whose name meant "my father rejoices," acted as a peacemaker. And as soon as the husband died, David married the delightful woman.

Yes, the meaning of biblical names can make the stories of Scripture much more interesting when we know what those proper nouns actually meant.

Beginning at least during the nineteenth century, biblical scholars used various new methodological tools in their interpretation of Scripture. They went by such terms as source criticism, redaction criticism, tradition criticism, form criticism, canon criticism, psychological criticism, etc. As we noted earlier, the word "criticism" is a technical term and does not necessarily connote something negative or disapproving. Scholars use it as a kind of synonym for a serious reading of the text. However, the overall result of such methods more often than not fractured Scripture, leaving conservative Christian and Jewish scholars feeling that the divine element of inspiration got completely thrown out because such methods seemed arbitrarily to rule out any supernatural element.

Beginning about 1980 a new form of study called narrative criticism got a jump start by Robert Alter's book *The Art of Biblical Narrative.* Narrative criticism (now often described as narrative theology) is basically a spin-off of literary criticism, which already played a longstanding role in nonbiblical studies. Soon narrative criticism came to be regarded as a legitimate academic discipline for biblical studies. And although narrative criticism doesn't necessarily reject the findings of the other methods of biblical research, it doesn't fragment Scripture but takes each story as a complete unit, probing the various dynamics within the received text itself. This approach in itself earns narrative theology more respect from conservative biblical scholars than they have for many of the older other scholarly approaches.

Philippe Mathieu, from the Leys School in Cambridge, England, describes narrative criticism: "It focuses on the literary characteristics of the text whilst ignoring any historical questions raised by the material. In other words the text is best treated as story with its own internal frame of reference."

Additionally, narrative criticism has been helpful because a working knowledge of the first-century ancient Near East is not a prerequisite for understanding the dynamics of the received biblical text. One can skillfully interpret scriptural narrative by being aware of the inner working dynamics of narrative writing.

I hope that you'll find the next several chapters insightful. Perhaps you'll learn things in some well-known Bible stories that you've never before noticed. If that's the case, don't let this new—and sometimes surprising—information overwhelm you. Read each story with an open mind.

CHAPTER 14

Story Time—The Akedah

K eeping in mind the ideas about understanding narrative presented
in the previous chapter, now let's look at some biblical stories and
see what we can learn from how the biblical author told them. As you
study these stories, which we'll examine in detail in this chapter and those
that follow, try to figure out who does the acting, who is acted upon, who
does the speaking, etc. Note the times and places mentioned in the stories—if they appear at all. See if you can agree with the insights presented
in these chapters.

I'll start out with a familiar story from the Old Testament—one that
Jews refer to as the Akedah. You may not know the story by that name,
but I know you're acquainted with the account in Genesis 22.

At the beginning of the story the patriarch Abraham was tenting in
Beer-sheba. As you know, he was not a Canaanite himself, but a
Mesopotamian. Born in Ur, Abram (his original name) moved with his
father, Terah, and family to Haran, also located in Mesopotamia. The Bible
tells us that Abraham's father was an idolater, along with other family
members (Joshua 24:2). Curiously, both Ur and Haran were centers for
worshipping the deity Sin, the moon god. At that time the moon god was
not especially popular in Mesopotamia, and there weren't a lot of cult centers for moon worship in that general area.

Nonetheless, the Person we call the "true God" (later known to the
Jews as YHWH) called Abraham to leave his native Mesopotamia and
move to a place that God Himself would show him. And Abraham's journey of many hundreds of miles landed him in Palestine, the land of
Canaan, where he "sojourned" and had to learn a new language.

The Canaanite language wasn't entirely foreign-sounding to Abraham, because it shared many features with his original Mesopotamian tongue. Canaanite (which, by the way, later came to be known as Hebrew) is classified today as a northwest Semitic language, just as Abraham's native tongue is. Perhaps the differences among the various northwest Semitic languages is somewhat similar to the variations among the Romance languages—French, Spanish, Portuguese, Italian, Romanian, and any other language derived from Latin.

God had promised Abraham that he would have "land" and so many descendants that they'd be like the stars or like sand on the seashore (Gen. 15:5; 22:17; cf. 17:2). Furthermore, all nations would be blessed through him (or bless themselves because of him, as the Hebrew says), whatever that means. God would be Abraham's deity, and Abraham and his offspring would be His people.

And for several decades it appeared that God was proficient in making promises to Abraham but deficient in keeping them. Abraham led a nomadic life in Palestine, wandering from place to place and camping on other people's land. Additionally, he and Sarah remained childless. Twice, though, they came up with a bright idea to remedy the situation.

First, Abraham told God that he thought that he should adopt his trusted servant, Eliezer, as heir. God didn't like the idea, insisting that the heir would be Abraham's own flesh and blood. Abraham asked the Lord to verify that His promise of land and many descendants would come to pass. So God cut a covenant with Abraham, passing through a series of dismembered animals, which implied that if His promises didn't come true, He Himself would suffer the same fate as those sacrificial creatures.

Second, Sarah proposed another idea. She urged Abraham to take Hagar, her servant girl, as a concubine. Maybe the young woman would be fertile, and, voilà, Abraham would have a flesh-and-blood heir. This time Abraham didn't bother to ask God what He thought of the idea. But 86-year-old Abraham seems to have liked the suggestion. And sure enough, the Egyptian girl gave birth to Ishmael—an heir! But God didn't approve of what Abraham had done.

Fourteen years later—when Abraham was 100 years old and Sarah was 90 (she'd already gone through menopause)—God finally fulfilled one of His promises with the birth of Isaac. But Abraham still didn't have a title deed to even one square inch of Canaanite real estate.

More time elapsed, and Abraham is tenting in Beer-sheba, in the land ruled by King Abimelech. (Note that I'm shifting to the present tense now as I relate the main details of this story.) And here's where the story of the Akedah begins.

The first scene in the story occurs at night, and God is the main actor and does most of the talking. (Abraham as costar in this scene has a bit role in which he says just one word.) The biblical author tells us at the outset that God came to test or tempt (Hebrew, *nacah*) the patriarch. The word means putting something to the test—examining it, as one might assay metal in order to verify its quality. The LXX (or Greek translation of Genesis) uses a form of the verb *peirázÿ*, which has the same basic meaning. But the word poses a problem for Christian interpreters. You see, the book of James warns Christians that they shouldn't say that God is testing them, because God tempts no one (James 1:13). We're tempted and tried by our own internal lusts—not by God (verse 14). James uses the very same Greek word in these verses— *peirázÿ*.

So exactly how was Abraham put to the test? Was it really God who was testing him—the deity James says tempts no one? Or was the source of Abraham's test his own innermost lusts, as James put it? And if the latter, then exactly what subjective psychological desire or innate drive would coerce a man to offer his son as a burnt sacrifice? There appears to be no easy answer here. Whichever alternative one opts for has unacceptable implications.

But back to the story. The ensuing conversation (Gen. 22:1, 2) sounds a bit choppy to us, but it sets the stage for the drama that will unfold throughout the rest of the chapter.

God: "Abraham."

Abraham: "Behold, here I am." (It is Abraham's single-word speech. He says simply *hinnênî* in Hebrew. Biblical Hebrew doesn't have a word that corresponds well with our "yes," as when we acknowledge someone speaking to us. The Hebrew word literally means "behold me.")

God: "Take now your son, your only son, whom you love, Isaac, and go to the land of Moriah; and offer him there as a burnt offering" (Gen. 22:2, NASB).

God gives an order with three verbs: "take," "go," and "offer." David

W. Cotter points out that the syntax here indicates that God is speaking quite politely to Abraham: "Would you take . . ." It's not really a question, of course. It's still a command, but not as harsh as the stark English rendering "take" makes it sound. In fact, some Jewish commentators have felt that the grammatical nuance here actually left Abraham with a choice—he really didn't have to "take, go, and offer." God was leaving him an out, so to speak (*Genesis,* Berit Olam: Studies in Hebrew Narrative and Poetry, p. 153).

And note the dramatic sequence that God uses to identify the person involved. "*Your* son." "Your *only* son." "Whom you *love*." And finally, "*Isaac*." The structure here tends to build suspense.

The first term could also refer to Ishmael, because he was Abraham's son too, but a son whom Abraham had sent packing, along with Hagar, years earlier. The second identifier is a bit deceiving at first—"only son." Mathematically Abraham had two sons, not just one, but only one of them was truly unique, a possible meaning of the Hebrew adjective *yachid.* The third term, "whom you love," uses for the first time in Scripture the Hebrew word for love. The fourth identifier is the son's proper name—Isaac. God leaves Abraham with no question as to whom He has in mind.

Isaac, the child of promise and the impossible baby—born to a 90-year-old postmenopausal woman—is to be the recipient of the action (the direct object, if you please) of two of the three verbs. Abraham is to *take* Isaac and *offer* him as a burnt offering. The worship of the ancient Hebrew people consisted of various kinds of offerings—meat offerings, wave offerings, heave offerings, drink offerings, sin offerings, peace offerings, trespass offerings, voluntary offerings, and burnt offerings. The noun God uses here is the technical term (*olah*) that refers to an offering completely incinerated, hence "burnt offering." (The term is sometimes translated by the English word "holocaust.") Nothing would be left at the end of the service.

End of dialogue.

In this first scene at least two missing elements strike the modern reader.

First, Sarah, Abraham's wife of so many decades, doesn't even have a cameo role—or in the entire narrative, for that matter. It's as though she has never been! It may well be that she had her own tent and so wasn't with Abraham when he received the message from God. But surely the next morning she would have wondered what Abraham was up to as he collected firewood and saddled (or bound the wood onto) a donkey in preparation for a trip that he, Isaac, and two servants would set out on momentarily.

True, it was a patriarchal society, so I suppose it was none of her business what Abraham was about to do. But Isaac was her son also, not just Abraham's. Surely it would have been appropriate for her to know what God had instructed her husband to do with Isaac—even though females were not allowed to participate in the actual offering of sacrifices.

Was it fair for Abraham to keep his wife in the dark about what he was planning to do—to travel for three days (or parts of three days), to climb Mount Moriah (wherever and whatever it was; some identify it with the Temple Mount in Jerusalem), and on that high place to slaughter their son of the promise, Isaac? God hadn't commanded Abraham to keep Sarah ignorant of the situation. It was Abraham's decision—and his alone—not to tell her.

Second, in this scene we find Abraham surprisingly acquiescent to God. His only reply was "hello." This man, who was quite capable of arguing with God, said nothing. Anyone familiar with the Abraham cycle of stories will find themselves caught by surprise at the sudden end of the conversation. One would expect that Abraham would protest to God—as he did when the Lord confided in him that Sodom was about to be destroyed, the city in which Lot, Abraham's nephew, now lived.

You remember how Abraham brashly remonstrated with God by reminding Him that the incineration of good people along with bad people was hardly Godlike. "That be far from thee to do after this manner, to slay the righteous with the wicked. . . . Shall not the Judge of all the earth do right?" (Gen. 18:25). Here we find Abraham lecturing the Deity on morality! The patriarch was rebuking God, because what He planned to do was not fair, not just, not righteous. "This is not becoming of You, God," Abraham said, giving God a verbal spanking.

And God wavered. No, actually He caved in to Abraham's demands. If Sodom had merely 10 good people in it, the Lord would spare the city.

But this night in Beer-sheba Abraham remains mum. Has the cat gotten his tongue? Has he lost his spunk, his moxie? Maybe he's simply too stunned to speak. God's current plan is far more shocking than what He did with Sodom. There, He was incinerating evildoers. Here, He is asking to be worshipped with a human sacrifice. Does Abraham regard God's proposed human burnt offering as not being out of harmony with His character? And so Abraham has no grounds for argument? (In later Israelite law God insisted that the firstborn son belonged to Him and had to be "redeemed" [Ex. 22:29; 34:19, 20].)

The offering of human sacrifice surely was not something Abraham had never heard of. We have evidence that it was done—at least on occasion—back in Mesopotamia. And it was a far more frequent rite performed by the Canaanites and later by the Phoenicians. So maybe Abraham didn't experience any cognitive dissonance here? We just don't know, and remain perplexed by the patriarch's silence.

The next morning the scene changes. Just as quickly and as mysteriously as God appeared to Abraham during the night, so He now disappears from the narrative. Abraham is now the main actor. Everyone else involved in the narrative is nearly invisible and pretty much mute—just as Abraham was the previous night when he'd had that nightmare (at least from our perspective).

"Abraham rose up early in the morning" (Gen. 22:3). The idea expressed here is that he is an early bird, who at the break of day is out of bed and ready for the day's activities. And like a whirlwind, he busies himself with the preparations. He saddles a male donkey, splits firewood, rounds up ("takes") Isaac and two servants, and sets out on the three-day expedition.

The third scene in the story finds the travelers in the general locale of Mount Moriah. Still at center stage, Abraham does all the acting. "Abraham lifted up his eyes, and saw the place afar off" (verse 4). Moriah may actually be a word play. It may come from a root word meaning "see" or "notice." So Abraham lifted up his eyes and "saw" the place of "seeing."

Next he instructs the servants to remain at this base camp, while he and Isaac would scale the mountain and worship there. Abraham chooses his words carefully, using plurals in reference to what he *and* Isaac would do. They would do three things together: climb the mountain, worship at its summit, and return. "I and the lad will go yonder and worship, and come again to you" (verse 5).

Here is an important nuance in the story—as we shall see later on. Abraham indicates that the two of them will climb the mountain, worship God, and then return—together. One would surmise that he would have said that *they*—the two of them—would ascend the mount and worship and that *he*—just Abraham—would descend from the place of worship. But that's not what he announces.

Abraham puts the bundle of fagots on Isaac's back and picks up a fire-pot (or firestone) and a knife (probably a meat cleaver) himself. And the two of them set off in this third scene of the story.

Abraham is 120 years old, so the hike is surely difficult for him. I can see him stopping from time to time to catch his breath. The climb for 20-year-old Isaac, of course, is hardly strenuous—even with the stack of firewood on his back. I see the son patiently standing by while his old father gasps for air. Once Abraham's pulse slows down to normal, or nearly normal, they continue their trek up the mountain.

Somewhere along the way Isaac decides to verbalize the question that has been running through his mind from the outset. "My father," he says gently.

"Here am I, my son."

"Behold the fire and the wood: but where is the lamb for a burnt offering?" (verse 7).

The narrator doesn't provide any insight into Isaac's thoughts and emotions, which is quite normal for Hebrew literary technique. In Hebrew narrative the story line consists chiefly of words and actions. (The same Hebrew term, *dabar*, can be translated either as "word" or "action," because words imply action.) The reader must infer affective insights from the words and actions presented.

Does Isaac think that maybe his old father has only a selective memory, remembering the sticks, the firestone, and the butcher knife but forgetting the sacrificial animal itself? Does the son have any inkling that *he* may be the intended victim? We simply don't know. Isaac's thoughts—like Abraham's—are not explicit. As readers we can only conjecture about them.

Abraham says something very strange in reply. He turns the sacrificial process backward. "My son, *God* will provide himself a lamb for a burnt offering," he replies. That's not the way it usually went. The worshipper brought the sacrificial animal—a gift to God. Here Abraham indicates that the Lord will supply the lamb (or goat)—a gift to (not from) the worshipper. That's nearly blasphemy! Who is going to worship whom here? When a human worships the divine, the human provides the animal. But if the divine supplies the animal, does that mean the Deity worships the human? Maybe Abraham is senile after all!

"So they went [walked on] both of them together" (verse 8). That's pretty sparse prose—just three Hebrew words. The Hebrew word translated "together" denotes union, oneness. The aged father and young adult son continue their journey in unison—in lockstep, maybe?

The end of the third scene brings us to the opening of the fourth. Abraham and Isaac are now atop Mount Moriah. "They came to the place which God had told him of" (verse 9). The father is still the star of the story. Isaac may be there with him, but in this scene the son does nothing and says nothing. The father does all the acting and speaking.

First, the narrative pictures the old patriarch as engaging in four distinct activities. "Abraham built an altar there, and laid the wood in order, and bound Isaac his son, and laid him on the altar upon the wood" (verse 9). He first erected (the Hebrew word can also mean "rebuild," so it's possible that an altar had once stood on this spot but had fallen into disuse) an altar, which surely took considerable effort, as the rocks must have been quite heavy. Maybe Isaac helped his father roll the stones into position, and then together they heaved them into place. But the biblical writer doesn't tell us about any activity on the son's part. He remains invisible and silent in scene four.

Once the altar is in place, Abraham places the kindling in an orderly manner atop it. The text stresses the neatness by repeating the same Hebrew root word that is first translated "laid" and then "in order." The story gives us no hint as to when exactly Abraham had removed the pile of fagots from Isaac's back. Had he done this before he'd built the altar or after? If after, then clearly Isaac wouldn't have been much help during the construction of the altar itself.

Next, Abraham ties his son. The Hebrew word for "bound" here is *'aqad*. And thus the Jewish name of this story: the Akedah, or alternatively the Aqedah—the binding (of Isaac). That Abraham has rope for tying up Isaac comes as a surprise. The narrator has not mentioned it elsewhere in the story. Maybe it was the same cord that had tied the kindling wood. And why Isaac might need to be trussed up is a bit of a mystery. He's been so compliant and even inactive throughout the narrative, one wonders why his father should restrain him with cords—as though he might resist.

Finally the father lays his son atop the wood, which in turn rested on the stone altar. The Hebrew verb here is not the same one used in describing how Abraham arranged the kindling in such an orderly manner. And what does Isaac—20-year-old Isaac—do? Nothing as far as we can tell. We read of no outbursts, no demanding of an explanation from his father, no fond farewells. Rather, we get no sense of emotion at all. Abraham merely goes about doing what is necessary to offer God worship with a burnt offering.

"And Abraham stretched forth his hand, and took the knife to slay his son" (verse 10). Usually we envision Abraham with his hand held aloft, ready to plunge a dagger into Isaac's chest. Maybe—maybe not. It's likely that a sacrificial animal was killed by slitting its throat. When Abraham extended his hand—freed his arm—he most likely was holding the honed edge of the meat cleaver to Isaac's throat, so that with a swift motion he could sever the jugular vein. Isaac would then quickly bleed to death.

"And the angel of the Lord called unto him out of heaven, and said, Abraham, Abraham" (verse 11).

The patriarch replied with his usual one word Hebrew response, "*Hinnênî*—Here *am* I" (verse 11).

The angel of YHWH instructed, "Lay not thine hand upon the lad, neither do thou any thing unto him: for now I know that thou fearest God, seeing thou hast not withheld thy son, thine only son from me" (verse 12).

In dramas such sudden, last-minute resolution came to be known as *deus ex machina* (pronounced DAY-us eks MOCK-ee-nah). In some ancient plays a god would be watching the action from above. When the hero came to his wits' end, the deity would rush in to resolve his predicament. This Latin term—itself a transliteration of a Greek expression—literally means "God out of a machine." In Greek and Roman dramas, for instance, at just the right moment an actor playing a god would be lowered onto the stage to rescue the hero. The role of the *deus ex machina* was to reward the virtuous protagonist and punish the villainous antagonist. Today the expression has taken on a pejorative connotation, referring to a too-facile (and even magical) way out of a problem, but originally people considered it to be a legitimate theatrical gambit.

A lot of discussion has concerned the identity of the angel of the Lord—the angel or messenger of YHWH. In verse 11 he appears to be distinct from YHWH Himself, but in verse 12 we hear YHWH's voice with the use of the pronoun "me." This shifting of perspectives from the angel of YHWH to YHWH Himself is not limited to this story. It happens elsewhere, which leads some interpreters to think that the angel of YHWH is a hypostasis (a stand-in or the very essence) of God Himself. Regardless, when the angel of YHWH speaks, he does so in behalf of God, and perhaps that's all we need to read into the evidence.

"And Abraham lifted up his eyes, and looked, and behold behind him a ram caught in a thicket by his horns: and Abraham went and took the ram, and offered him up for a burnt offering in the stead of his son" (verse 13). The narrative tension that has been building from verse 1 is now released. But once again we gain no insights into Abraham's or Isaac's state of mind—the profound sense of relief that they must have individually experienced. We read about no exhalations of breath, no muttering of "Whew!" And strange as it may seem, God *did* provide an animal for the burnt offering—contrary to the usual procedure in which a human supplied the creature as a gift to God. (Interestingly, at least two figurines of a goat caught in a bush have been unearthed at ancient Ur—eerily prescient of the animal provided in this story.)

But the aftermath of the biblical narrative is unsettling. It's almost as though this test fractured Abraham's family. Let me explain.

Abraham had earlier told his servants that "we" will return after having worshipped atop Mount Moriah. That is a significant point. However, despite the ram that God provided for the sacrifice, the narrative tells us that "Abraham returned unto his young men" (verse 19). It doesn't say that he *and* Isaac returned. In fact, it doesn't even use the plural pronoun "they" in reference to Abraham and Isaac. According to the text, only Abraham returns to the young men. "And they [Abraham and his servants] rose up and went together to Beer-sheba; and Abraham dwelt at Beer-sheba" (verse 19).

So the story begins at Beer-sheba and ends there. It was at Beer-sheba that God had asked Abraham to offer Isaac as a burnt offering; it was from Beer-sheba that Abraham, Isaac, and the two servants had traveled; and it was back to Beer-sheba that Abraham and his two servants returned after the ordeal.

Did Abraham actually offer Isaac along with the ram God provided? That's hardly the case, because in Genesis 24 Abraham sends his servant to find a wife for Isaac, and Isaac and Rebekah marry, living happily ever after. But note the following strange bit of information: Isaac was living at Beer-lahai-roi (Gen. 24:62). Archaeologists have not located the exact site, but it's somewhere between the cities of Kadesh and Bered.

The narrator tells us that Abraham returned to Beersheba and that Isaac was living in the vicinity of Beer-lahai-roi. But that's not all.

In the chapter immediately following the narrative of the Akedah, Sarah dies—at the age of 127 years. (Sarah died 17 years after the Akedah, but the account of her death immediately follows the Akedah story. Some ancient Jewish scholars proposed that when she heard about what Abraham had done, she screamed in anguish . . . and died. But the chronology of events disagrees with such an idea.) And where was she when she died? Sarah was at Hebron, known at that time as Kiriath-arba. "And Abraham came to mourn for Sarah" (Gen. 23:2). In her old age Sarah dies at Kiriath-arba, where Abraham arrives to weep over her. But where did he travel from? One presumes that he came from Beer-sheba, where he'd returned after his experience atop Mount Moriah.

It was at Kiriath-arba that Abraham obtained his first piece of real estate in Canaan—the Cave of Machpelah. But he acquired this property the same way most of us get ours—he purchased it. And it wasn't cheap, either! He paid Ephron the Hittite 400 shekels of silver (verse 16) for the cave and the surrounding land.

What can we make of these details? Abraham in Beer-sheba, Isaac in the vicinity of Beer-lahai-roi, and Sarah at Kiriath-arba (Hebron)? Did the Akedah lead to the breakup of Abraham's family? We just don't know.

Excursus on Divine Omniscience

When YHWH interrupted Abraham from performing his grisly act of worship, He announced to the patriarch, "Now I know that thou fearest God" (Gen. 22:12). What is the implication of His comment?

Some commentators regard it as anthropomorphic language that we should not take literally. God knows everything, they state, so one must understand God's own statement here as symbolic language. Such assertions, of course, assume that the theologians are smart enough to know what God knows and does not know—even though He Himself declared through Isaiah that His ways are far higher than ours (Isa. 55:8, 9). And the apostle Paul centuries later wrote that God's "ways [are] past finding out!" (Rom. 11:33). So it takes a certain amount of hubris to assert boldly that God can or cannot do this or that or know this or that.

This commonly accepted (and often unquestioned) theological perspective argues that God has exhaustive (total) knowledge of not only the past and present but also of the future. As a result, He knows in advance—from eternity, actually—who will be saved and who will be lost. Such knowledge lets Him know from eternity what color socks I'll wear today, tomorrow, and forever. He knows in advance—from eternity, actually—what I'll buy at Wal-Mart throughout my entire existence. And He knows in advance every time that I will choose to clear my throat for the rest of my life.

It depends on one's school of thought as to *how and why* God has such comprehensive foreknowledge.

According to Calvinistic theology, God's omniscience is based on His absolute sovereignty. God in His perfect and absolute control has decreed from eternity past everything that will ever take place on Planet Earth, including the use of the will made by each human being. Thus God knows the future perfectly and extensively and fully because He knows that what He Himself has decreed will occur—and that's everything that has happened, is happening, and will ever happen. John Calvin recognized that this is a difficult doctrine to accept, but he believed that he had sufficient scriptural evidence to warrant an all-encompassing predestination. We sometimes referred to this concept as "hard Calvinism."

In short, there is a cause-and-effect relationship between God's omniscience (or perhaps more properly His omnipotence) and our behavior. His eternal divine decrees are the cause of everything that happens on Planet Earth, including human behavior, whether it's good or bad. Yes, according to Calvin, God decreed that Adam and Eve would sin. It was what He wanted!

Another explanation in defense of God's totally complete foreknowledge does not necessarily share all the presuppositions of Calvinism. Theologians holding this perspective view God's absolute foreknowledge as based on His eternity. God is eternal, they argue, which means that He exists outside of time—unlike His finite and temporal creatures. Because He is external to time, not embedded in it, He sees before Him past, present, and future in one seamless whole. So divine foreknowledge doesn't cause human behavior, but it has a correlation with the choices made by the will, and that's all. Just as blue eyes have a correlation with blond hair but don't cause light-colored hair, so God's perfect knowledge has a correlation with human use of free will but doesn't cause that exercise of free will.

Nonetheless, even this correlative approach between the interplay of divine omniscience and human free will stumbles at Genesis 22:12 and other similar biblical passages. Two questions can point this up: (1) How *extensive* is God's knowledge based on His existing outside of time? and (2) How *precise* is His knowledge based on His existing outside of time? If the answer to both questions is "completely" or something similar, as it most likely will be, then regardless of the correlative relationship, the activities that God foresees are indeed truly inevitable. The foreseen events (which include everything that occurs) *must* happen—else God's knowledge is *not* extensive and is *not* precise, which turns out to be an unacceptable option to theologians who hold this position.

So the end result is the same whether one holds to a causative relationship between God's omniscience and human free will or whether one holds to a correlative relationship between His omniscience and human free will. Each instance of human behavior is inevitable—either because God omnipotently decreed it or because He perfectly foresaw it.

Other theologians take the language of Genesis 22:12 literally. They point out that as verse 1 indicates, the incident was a test, but we didn't learn at the story's opening exactly what kind of test it was. Now in verse 12 we find out. The result of the test wasn't for Abraham's sake—it was for God's. Until now, the Lord assumed that Abraham trusted Him—feared Him. But the patriarch's behavior prior to the Akedah was a bit spotty, marked by his own double attempts to get an heir and even some lies he had spoken to Pharaoh and Abimelech.

Walter Brueggemann, an Old Testament scholar, observes: "Verse 1 sets the test, suggesting God wants to know something. . . . It is not a game with God. God genuinely does not know. And that is settled in verse 12, 'Now I know'" (*Genesis*, Interpretation: A Bible Commentary, p. 187).

"God's statement, 'now I know,' raises serious theological problems regarding divine immutability and foreknowledge. . . . It is often suggested that the test was for Abraham's benefit, not God's. It should be noted, however, that the only one in the text said to learn anything from the test is *God*. . . . If one presupposes that God already 'knew' the results of the test beforehand, then the text is at least worded poorly and at most simply false" (John Sanders, *The God Who Risks: A Theology of Providence*, p. 52).

Bible scholars call this theological perspective "presentism," but it's also commonly known as "openness of God" theology. (Some label it "process theology," but technically that's a quite different sort of theology.) But how do these theologians relate to the divine attribute of omniscience? The same way they do God's omnipotence.

Back in the 1200s Thomas Aquinas argued that God's omnipotence means that He can do all that is an object of power—that is, something that it is not impossible to do. Some things, however, are not objects of power and are, thereby, even impossible for God. God cannot remember our sins when He says He'll forget them or make a rock so big that He cannot move it. Despite His omnipotence, He cannot make 2 + 3 = 7 or construct a triangle with four sides and four 90-degree interior angles.

Similarly, presentist theologians reason that God cannot know that which is not an object of knowledge—that which it is forever impossible to know. God cannot know that black is white, for instance. And He cannot know with precision exactly how beings with free will might choose in every circumstance. Certainly He would have a good idea of how Mary might choose, because He has watched her since her birth and knows her habit and thought patterns better than anyone else. Nonetheless, she has the ability and the freedom to choose in a way that can surprise even God.

As a result, such theologians do not have to "explain away" scriptural passages such as Genesis 22:12. They feel quite comfortable in understanding them literally. However, perhaps the strongest argument against this alternative view, which is gaining in popularity among evangelical Christians, is *fulfilled* biblical prophecy. Note that I've used the modifier "fulfilled." (You'll understand why a bit later.) If God's omniscience is not all-encompassing and perfectly accurate for all behavior, how is it that God can predict the future? What about all those fulfilled predictions of biblical prophecy?

However, God was quite explicit with Isaiah about how it is that He can predict events to come. "Hast thou not heard long ago, how I have done it; and of ancient times, that I have formed it? now have *I brought it to pass*" (Isa. 37:26). "Yea, I have spoken it, *I will also bring it to pass*" (Isa. 46:11). "I have declared the former things from the beginning; and they went forth out of my mouth, and I shewed them; *I did them suddenly,* and they came to pass" (Isa. 48:3).

Did you notice what Scripture offers as the fundamental reason why God can foretell future events? Because He Himself works to bring them to pass. But we must carefully note that He doesn't say that He works to make all events happen, so He's not really a Calvinist. He does operate behind the scenes, though, when necessary to mold human history. Fulfilled prophecy is evidence that God is at work—doing what He said He would do. (See Daniel 10:13, 20, in which God's messenger to Daniel has come from and will return to the king of Persia to influence his behavior.)

There's a flip side to this matter of prophecy. It comes as a surprise to many people to learn that the Bible also has unfulfilled prophecies that never came to pass and probably never will.

For example, we're all familiar with the story of Jonah, the prophet swallowed by a huge fish as he was running away from responsibility. He finally ended up at Nineveh despite his best efforts to flee in the opposite direction. Jonah predicted the destruction of Nineveh in 40 days, but nothing happened. The people exercised their free will and repented, and God spared them.

God told Ezekiel that He was fed up with Tyre and would destroy the city. "Behold, I am against thee, O Tyrus, and will cause many nations to come up against thee, as the sea causeth his waves to come up. And they shall destroy the walls of Tyrus, and break down her towers: I will also scrape her dust from her, and make her like the top of a rock. It shall be a place for the spreading of nets in the midst of the sea: for I have spoken it" (Eze. 26:3-5).

God even named the king who would conquer Tyre. "I will bring upon Tyrus Nebuchadrezzar king of Babylon. . . . He shall slay with the sword thy daughters in the field: and he shall make a fort against thee, and cast a mount against thee, and lift up the buckler against thee. And he shall set engines of war against thy walls, and with his axes he shall break down thy towers. . . . Thy walls shall shake at the noise of the horsemen, and of the wheels, and of the chariots, when he shall enter into thy gates. . . . He shall slay thy people by the sword. . . . They shall break down thy walls, and destroy thy pleasant houses: and they shall lay thy stones and thy timber and thy timber and thy dust in the midst of the water" (verses 7-12).

But Nebuchadnezzar's siege failed, so God later told Ezekiel that He was going to give Egypt to Nebuchadnezzar as a consolation prize. "Son of man, Nebuchadrezzar king of Babylon caused his army to serve a great service against Tyrus: every head was made bald, and every shoulder was peeled: yet had he no wages, nor his army, for Tyrus, for the service that he had served against it: therefore thus saith the Lord God; Behold, I will give the land of Egypt unto Nebuchadrezzar king of Babylon" (Eze. 29:18, 19). "Thus saith the Lord God; I will also make the multitude of Egypt to cease by the hand of Nebuchadrezzar king of Babylon" (Eze. 30:10).

Somehow human free will and diligent effort on the part of the Tyrians led to the failure of God's prediction through Ezekiel that King Nebuchadnezzar would utterly destroy the city. It didn't happen, and even God admitted that it hadn't occurred.

CHAPTER 15

Story Time—Samson

An author has many options to choose from the storehouse of plots or patterns to organize or structure a story. The Bible employs many of them. But in this chapter we will look at a very ancient one that has appeared throughout history and in almost every culture. One might argue that the human brain is hardwired in such a way that storytellers worldwide come up with this particular story line independently of one another. The details that embellish the plot can differ from one permutation to the next, making each story unique, but the essential story line remains pretty much the same. That does not mean that the plot has never happened in real life. Rather, it is a certain way of seeing events, of finding in them specific patterns. People can look at the same body of actual facts and incidents and view and arrange them in different ways. For example, Abraham Lincoln lived a historically verifiable life. But different biographers regard that life as illustrating different themes. They may view it as an example of someone triumphing over hardship and failure or as illustrating certain social, economic, and historical forces and trends in his time and world.

As we have mentioned, some of these patterns that people see around them are quite old and widespread. We will look at one ancient example. What follows are some of the foremost components of this pattern or plot: (1) imminent danger threatens to change stability—law and order—into chaos; (2) someone in authority—king, queen, God—assigns a hero to rectify the state of affairs; (3) the protagonist is provided with potent equipment for the task; (4) the hero penetrates enemy lines, where he or she executes the dangerous mission; (5) the hero encounters various life-endangering close calls; (6) by utilizing the powerful—even magical—gear granted to him or her, the protagonist saves the day; and (7) the champion returns home victorious, ready to be commissioned for another hair-raising assignment.

The James Bond movies, despite their various transformations of story line, pretty much follow the superhero plot outline given above: (1) some evil person or power threatens the security of the free world; (2) British secret service headquarters dispatches James Bond, Agent 007 with a "license to kill," to resolve the problem; (3) the research-and-development team provides Bond with astounding offensive and defensive equipment; (4) Agent 007, through a series of harrowing adventures, infiltrates the territory of the adversary; (5) once in place, James Bond encounters additional misadventures—often as a result of his dalliances with enemy women; (6) by utilizing both his fighting prowess and special gadgetry, Bond manages to survive (pretty much miraculously) the nefarious menaces to his life—one escapade after another; and (7) having saved the free world by routing the forces of evil, Agent 007 returns home to England.

Samson—An Ancient Hebrew James Bond

Ian Fleming, author of the James Bond series of books, didn't invent this story line; he merely utilized a standardized plot or literary pattern that has intrigued both storytellers and audiences around the world throughout history. He, along with contemporary movie scriptwriters, have fun incorporating high-tech gear for Bond—equipment that often is just beyond what modern technology can accomplish but not that far advanced that it's totally unbelievable. And throughout the story one hears countless puns—often in the names of the enemy's people, including Bond's lovers—as well as sarcastic remarks passed off as wry humor. And, surprisingly, it is also what a careful reader meets in the Samson stories of Judges 13-16. (As we look at the Samson narrative we will also employ some of the insights we have gained in previous chapters.)

In approximately 150 places the Old Testament called certain individuals *gibbor* (*gibborim*—plural). The Hebrew terminology described men of valor/courage—gutsy warriors who undertook great feats of bravery. Although he is not specifically called a *gibbor*, we can rightfully classify Samson among them. The biblical writer recounts his story in four acts,

165

which we'll now look at carefully. Each act features a woman who, like Samson, is a main actor in the story.

Act 1—Woman Number 1—For 40 years the Philistines had been harassing the Israelites, who had been behaving badly (Judges 13:1). The Hebrew word used to describe their behavior is *ra*, which describes actions so offensive that they disturb the peace. Scripture isn't specific here as to exactly what sort of misbehavior the Hebrew people had engaged in (perhaps idolatry), but whatever it was, as a result they came under the thumb of the Philistine people, suffering for several decades.

Like the Israelites, the Philistines were not indigenous to Canaan. They had invaded the coastland (the Egyptians called them "Peoples of the Sea") and took up residence on Canaan's maritime plain. (The Hebrew people had settled pretty much in the hill country.) Although Scripture indicates that some Philistines lived in Canaan during the time of Abraham, they overran Palestine (named after them) not all that long before Samson's birth. They appear to have pretty much adopted Canaanite practices, and they had settled into five chief strongholds: Ekron, Gaza, Ashkelon, Ashdod, and Eglon. From this time to when David became king, they were the chief disturbers of Israelite peace.

One Israelite town atop one of the Judean foothills was called Zorah ("place of hornets") and was in the territory absorbed by the tribe of Dan. Place of Hornets was about 15 miles west of Jerusalem. After the time of Samson, when the Philistines returned on the warpath, the Danites abandoned the settlement and moved to a place called Laish, which they renamed Dan. (Remember the biblical expression "from Dan to Beer-sheba?") The name "Place of Hornets" makes one wonder if the town might have been less than delightful! Indeed, if we take the name literally—and why should we not?—the earliest settlers here must have at times found themselves driven nearly crazy by the angry attacks of stinging wasps.

Here lived Mr. Rest Secure (that's what Manoah means) and his wife, who has no name in this story, although she plays the first major role in the narrative. The wife had been childless—a disaster for Hebrew wives, who when barren were regarded as insubordinate, stubborn "fields" that rejected the "seed" implanted by the husband when he "plowed" them. With no children, the couple had no help with family chores. And with no sons, the family name (and concomitant honor) and real estate would eventually fade away.

One day an angel from YHWH came to Mrs. Rest Secure and said, "You shall conceive and bear a son" (verse 3, NRSV). As you may recall, here we have another common motif or literary pattern among Hebrew stories about famous people—a childless woman gives birth to a son who becomes renowned. The news must have been very exciting for Mrs. Rest Secure, even though death during childbirth cut short the life of countless women in the ancient Near East.

Mrs. Rest Secure also received instruction as to how she should live during her pregnancy: "Drink not wine nor strong drink, and eat not any unclean thing" (verse 4).

Apparently it was not unusual for women to drink alcoholic beverages back then—even among the Israelites. Both wine and beer, of course, could be intoxicating. Wine was typically diluted before it was imbibed, but people drank beer straight, which made it more potent than wine. The Philistines were famous for their consumption of beer, and archaeologists have uncovered numerous beer mugs with built-in strainers in Philistine cities and villages. Beer in the ancient world was nearly as much a staple as was bread—both supplying many calories for diets that could be otherwise low in nutritional value.

Also Mrs. Rest Secure was to abstain from eating unclean foods. One wonders why it was necessary to instruct a Hebrew woman to keep a kosher home. Readers can logically infer that not all Israelites adhered to the requirements of Leviticus 11. Whether that resulted from necessity or choice, we really don't know.

But the messenger sent by YHWH (remember what we said about the "angel of YHWH" in the previous chapter?) had yet another surprise. Scholars do not all agree as to how we should translate the message. The grammar used can be translated as "Actually, you are already pregnant and bearing a son" (verse 5, Anchor). Most, however, continue using the future tense: "You will become pregnant, bearing a son." If the former translation, as given by Robert G. Boling, is correct, then Mrs. Rest Secure gets a double surprise: The angel tells her first that she will give birth and then corrects himself a few moments later by stating that she is already pregnant.

Then came another zinger for Mrs. Rest Secure: "The boy shall be a nazirite to God from birth" (verse 5, NRSV). The Hebrew word *nazir* means dedicated to God. Not only was Mother to live as a Nazirite during her nine months of pregnancy, but the child was also to be a Nazirite. In fact, the newborn was to be a perpetual Nazirite—from birth to death (verses 5 and 7). Nazirites were men or women who took a vow that stipulated they (1) would not ingest anything from the grapevine, (2) would not cut their hair, and (3) would not touch any dead thing. The concept of being a Nazirite seems to be related to the state of ritual purity that Hebrew soldiers were to maintain while on duty.

And yet another bombshell hurtled her way. (How many surprises could a person take? First, a barren woman learned that she'd become pregnant. Second, she actually was already pregnant. Third, she would give birth to a son. Fourth, she should become a Nazirite during the pregnancy. Fifth, her baby boy must be a Nazirite from his delivery to his funeral.) The angel concluded, "It is he who shall begin to deliver Israel from the hand of the Philistines" (verse 5, NRSV). This child from tiny Place of Hornets would initiate the Israelite emancipation from Philistine tyranny, which ultimately King David himself would complete centuries later.

Excited with this good news, the wife—and soon-to-be mother—ran to her husband (Manoah—Mr. Rest Secure) to share the almost unbelievable tidings. She told him what this man from God (she didn't identify him as an *angel* of YHWH) had announced to her (verses 6, 7).

Mr. Rest Secure didn't jump up and down with excitement. Instead, he didn't seem to know what to make of his wife's report. But, being the religious man that he was, he offered up a prayer: "O, Lord, I pray, let the man of God whom you sent come to us again and teach us what we are to do concerning the boy who will be born" (verse 8, NRSV). Not having seen the divine messenger, the husband used the same terminology that his wife had used—"a *man* of God."

The narrator tells us that God answered the prayer, again sending "the *angel* of God" (verse 9). But rather than commissioning the angel to Mr. Rest Secure, God once again dispatched him to Mrs. Rest Secure—a strange way of answering the husband's prayer! But she ran to let her husband know that "the man" had returned, and both husband and wife rushed back to the field where the epiphany had taken place, for the second time, to Mrs. Rest Secure. Interestingly, the wife led the way, with the husband trailing behind. (Mr. Rest Secure is too much at rest in this story, too much at ease, too laid-back!)

With the husband on the scene, the wife no longer needed to speak. In fact, it's quite amazing that the woman spoke at all in the story. All too often in Hebrew narrative the women remain mum while the men do all the talking. "Are you the man who spoke to this woman?" (verse 11, NRSV), Mr. Rest Secure asked.

The messenger didn't correct Mr. Rest Secure by indicating that he really wasn't a man but an angel. He simply responded to the question positively.

"Now let thy words come to pass. How shall we order the child, and how shall we do unto him?" (verse 12). What, was this a mail-order baby? "How shall we order" is what it says in the Hebrew, but the idea is "What rules shall be observed for the boy?" (Tanakh). Having a baby was a totally new experience for the couple, and on top of that, from infancy to death the child was to be a Nazirite.

The angel—not the man—repeated the instructions that he'd previously given to the woman.

Showing the hospitality so common in the ancient Near East (and even today), Mr. Rest Secure invited the "man" to stay for a meal. The "angel" replied, "If you detain me, I will not eat your food; but if you want to prepare a burnt offering, then offer it to the Lord" (verse 16, NRSV).

Mr. Rest Secure then asked the individual for his name, though he was so shaken by the turn of events that he used improper grammar when addressing him. But the messenger replied that since his name was secret or unknowable—beyond comprehension—why did Mr. Rest Secure want to know it? (Incidentally, here we have the noun form of the same word used in Isaiah 9:6: "For unto us a child is born, unto us a son is given: and the government shall be upon his shoulder: and his name shall be called *Wonderful*, Counsellor, The mighty God, The everlasting Father, The Prince of Peace.")

Mr. Rest Secure offered a kid and a meal offering to YHWH, and while the flames ascended, the angel jumped into the fire and "ascended in the flame of the altar" (Judges 13:20, NRSV). In awe, Mr. and Mrs. Rest Secure prostrated themselves. The angel went up, and the husband

and wife went down! (We find a lot of going up and going down else-where in this amazing story. Biblical writers loved to use such patterns.)

Now much wiser than at the outset of the story, Mr. Rest Secure ac-knowledged that it was no mere man whom they'd encountered. No, he was indeed an angel—an angel of YHWH. And once this realization had sunk in, Mr. Rest Secure became paranoid. "We shall surely die, for we have seen God" (verse 22, NRSV), he whined.

But Mrs. Rest Secure wasn't so wimpy. She told her husband, "If the Lord had meant to kill us, he would not have accepted a burnt offering and a grain offering at our hands, or shown us all these things, or now an-nounced to us such things as these" (verse 23, NRSV). Level-headed, the wife of Mr. Rest Secure was!

The first act of the story, which revolves around Mrs. Rest Secure, ends with the announcement of the child's birth and naming—she called him Samson, which, as we noted previously, probably means something like Sunny. "The boy grew, and the Lord blessed him" (verse 24, NRSV). But that's not all. "The spirit of the Lord began to stir him" (verse 25, NRSV). This last statement presages the commissioning that Sunny re-ceived from God.

Act 1 is now over, and it was a humdinger of one—full of suspense and surprises!

Act 2—*Woman Number 2*—We now meet the second woman in the story about Sunny, who is now a young adult. He went "down" from his home in Place of Hornets to a little town called Timnath or Timnah ("al-lotted portion"). Topographically this is accurate, because Zorah ("place of hornets") is at an elevation of 1,170 feet, whereas the elevation of Timnah ("allotted portion") has an elevation of only 800 feet. The town name seems to serve as a pun, because the concept of allotment seems to lie just under the surface of Act 2.

While down in Philistine territory, Sunny met a woman who caught his eye. After he'd come back up to his home, he said to his parents, "I saw a Philistine woman at Timnah; now get her for me as my wife" (Judges 14:2, NRSV).

The news must have come as a terrible shock to Mr. and Mrs. Rest Secure. The ideal Hebrew marriage was endogamous, which means that one married within the clan—relatives. For example, "Abraham married his half sister (Gen. 20:12); Nahor married his brother's daughter, his niece (Gen. 11:29); Isaac married his father's brother's son's daughter, his first cousin's daughter (Gen. 24:15); Esau, among others, married his father's brother's daughter, his paternal parallel cousin (Gen. 28:9); Jacob married his mother's brother's daughters, his maternal parallel cousins (Gen. 29:10); Amram, Moses' father, married his father's sister, his paternal aunt (Ex. 6:20; Num. 26:57-59)" (Bruce J. Malina, *The New Testament World*, p. 105).

But Sunny's marriage would be exogamous—marrying outside the clan. For us today we would consider exogamy the norm. Indeed, endogamy is against the law. But not so in Israelite society. Besides, the young woman was a Philistine—a pagan. She didn't worship YHWH. So Sunny's parents asked, "Is there not a woman among your kin, or among all our people, that you must go to take a wife from the uncircumcised Philistines?" (Judges 14:3, NRSV). (As far as modern scholarship can tell, the Philistines were the only uncircumcised people living in Canaan at that time. The Hebrew term to describe them is "foreskinned ones.")

Sunny wouldn't be deterred, and with unusual brazenness he gave his parents a command: "Get her for me, because she pleases me" (verse 3, NRSV). Literally, he describes this woman (not a girl, so perhaps a widow) as the one who "looks right to me," which is not all that different from "she pleases me."

The parents—namely, the father—had to "get" the woman, because it was a time of arranged marriages. Marriages weren't just simple romantic arrangements in which boy meets girl and falls in love with girl and marries girl. Mr. Rest Secure would need to negotiate with the woman's family. He would have to produce a bride price that all agreed was fair. The woman's father would have to pull together a dowry. Wedding plans would then have to be arranged for the betrothed couple.

At this point it's tempting to write off Sunny as a spoiled brat who wanted his way regardless of his family's wishes. And that may be the case—at least in part. But the narrator clues us in on a well-kept secret: "[YHWH] was seeking a pretext to act against the Philistines" (verse 4, NRSV). The Hebrew word translated here as "pretext"—*ta'anah*—can be translated as "the right moment." Scripture also used it to describe the "heat" that a female entered when she was eager for sex. YHWH was looking for the time when the Philistines would be in heat for destruction.

That explanation may tend to get Sunny off the hook, but it just might cause more troubling questions than it alleviates. Why would God Himself want an Israelite—a Nazirite, at that—to marry a pagan Philistine? Elsewhere God forbade such marriages. It may be true that He wanted to teach the Philistines a lesson, but does the end justify the means? The biblical story never asks or answers that question, so we must leave it here. What we do learn from this inside information, though, is that YHWH was specially commissioning Sunny.

So, the narrator tells us, Mr. Rest Secure, Mrs. Rest Secure, and Sunny make the trek down to Allotted Portion—presumably to negotiate betrothal plans. What we read next is a bit puzzling. Suddenly we find Sunny all by himself in the vineyards just outside Allotted Portion. What a Nazirite was doing in the vineyards is anyone's guess. The author doesn't provide any clues. Suddenly a lion—not a cub, but a young, virile lion—attacked him, roaring as only they can do.

Readers would assume that Sunny would turn and run (a bad thing to do when a lion attacks) or would fall down and play dead (also a bad thing to do in such situations). Sunny did neither. "The spirit of the Lord rushed on him, and he tore the lion apart barehanded as one might tear apart a kid" (verse 6, NRSV).

This is our first glimpse of his prodigious strength. With his bare hands he ripped the lion apart as if it were a kid. The text is ambiguous in its description of Sunny's behavior. Did he tear apart the lion in the same manner that the lion would have done to a baby goat? Did he rend the lion as though the lion were a baby goat? It really doesn't matter. Either way, Sunny—when possessed by the Spirit of YHWH—had unparalleled muscle power.

At this point I begin to envision him as a huge hulk of a man—like those on television competing to win the "World's Strongest Man" title. I imagine his neck as having the circumference of some girls' waists! I see his upper arms bulked up like tree trunks and his forearms as big as . . . perhaps he was like Arnold Schwarzenegger on steroids. But maybe that wasn't the case. The Bible tells us that Sunny performed such "impossible" feats of strength when the "spirit of the Lord came mightily upon him" (verse 6; cf. verses 19 and Judges 15:14).

From there in the vineyards—apparently Sunny was still en route to his girlfriend's house—he went inside the town and visited with his unnamed lady love, and "she pleased Samson" (Judges 14:7, NRSV). As far as he was concerned, she was still the one—the right one.

Well, a year elapsed—most betrothals lasted that long—and it was time for the wedding gala. On the way down to the town of Allotted Portion, Sunny once again stepped into the nearby vineyards, and he found the carcass of the lion that he had killed some 12 months earlier. Some honeybees had built a hive in it. And there was a honeycomb in the carrion.

Now, a Nazirite was to avoid dead bodies, but Sunny apparently forgot his ritual status and scooped up some of the honeycomb in his hands. And as he sauntered along toward his betrothed's house, he snacked on the dripping sweetness, probably licking his fingers as he walked along. By the way, among the Israelites, rumor had it that honey could make a man strong and courageous. But Sunny certainly didn't need to eat any! He was already a daredevil.

Finally he made it to the house, where his parents and future in-laws were waiting. He even shared the honey in the comb with his mother and father, keeping them in the dark as to where he'd obtained it. Can't you just see his parents gagging had they known its source?

Wedding time came, and Sunny threw a drinking party that would last for seven days for the guests. Yes, that's what the Hebrew word means. Ummm, wasn't Sunny supposed to be a Nazirite? What was a Nazirite doing throwing a drinking party?

The Philistines wanted to honor him, so they assigned 30 men to accompany him during the seven days of the drinking bout. Then Sunny had a bright idea. Why not challenge them with a riddle? Riddle-solving was an ancient form of entertainment, so it sounded like a good idea. If one of the 30 Philistines could solve the riddle, Sunny would provide them with 30 linen tunics and 30 changes of wardrobe. And if they couldn't crack the riddle by the end of the seven-day drinking party, then they would have to give him the same prize.

The riddle? "Out of the eater came forth meat, and out of the strong came forth sweetness" (see verse 14).

Sunny was quite devious here. It may have sounded like a riddle, but it was really a description of what had actually happened to him when he was alone. Not even his mother and father knew about the fight with the lion and the existence of the honeycomb inside its remains. (One wonders why he never mentioned the incident to them.) A riddle such as this would be impossible to crack, and Sunny felt pretty good about himself. He'd best the 30 Philistines and get enough clothing to last him a lifetime! (Clothing was extremely time-consuming and expensive to make. Unlike moderns with their overstuffed closets, few ancients owned more than one or two changes of garment.)

And sure enough, the 30 Philistines found themselves stumped. They cracked every brain cell they had for three days, but to no avail. Now their honor was at stake. If they couldn't solve the riddle, they'd lose face and have to come up with 30 tunics plus 30 garments for Sunny. But they had no intention of doing that here in the town of Allotted Portion. They would not allot that portion of clothing to a Hebrew wise guy!

By the fourth day the 30 Philistines were getting desperate. So they approached Sunny's bride, saying, "Coax your husband to explain the riddle to us" (verse 15, NRSV). They wanted her to lure him into spilling the beans to her privately so that she could then relay the solution to the riddle to her fellow countrymen.

The Hebrew word used here means to be wide open and/or to seduce. It can have sexual overtones, and Scripture uses it that way. "And if a man entice a maid that is not betrothed, and lie with her, he shall surely endow her to be his wife" (Ex. 22:16). Note that word "entice," the same term used in our present story. In short, they wanted the new bride to use her sexual prowess to charm Sunny into revealing to her the secret to the riddle.

The Philistines were really playing hardball here, because they ended with a threat. "Or we will burn you and your father's house with fire" (Judges 14:15, NRSV).

For the rest of the week the bride cajoled and badgered him by questioning his devotion. With tears she accused, "You hate me; you do not really love me" (verse 16, NRSV). When she pleaded with him to tell her the solution, he explained that even his parents didn't know it (verse 16).

But the nagging and simpering and weeping eventually wore Sunny down. On the last day he finally gave in, explaining how he had killed the lion and later found a honeycomb in the carrion. Promptly she shared the solution with the 30 Philistines.

Just "before the sun went down" (verse 18, NRSV) on the seventh day of the feast (was it the Sabbath?), the Philistine men informed Sunny that they knew the answer to his riddle, and they presented it through a set of questions—a kind of riddle: "What is sweeter than honey? What is stronger than a lion?" (verse 18, NRSV).

Sunny, of course, was not amused. "If you had not plowed with my heifer, you would not have found out my riddle" (verse 18, NRSV). Suddenly this woman who had been "right" for him he now referred to as a heifer—a cow. Not very flattering. I hope that she didn't overhear him!

We may have a wry double entendre here. Is Sunny saying not only that the 30 Philistines had collaborated with his bride to do him wrong but also that they had engaged in an adulterous affair with her?

Just at that moment the Spirit of YHWH rushed upon Sunny, and the retribution began! He headed for Ashkelon, about 25 miles distant. It would take most men seven or eight hours to make the trip—one way. When Sunny got there, he slaughtered 30 of its men, stripped them naked, and returned to Allotted Portion with the Philistines' allotted portion of clothing. Sunny was a man of his word!

Then . . . well, the honeymoon was over—after only seven days. "In hot anger he went back to his father's house" (verse 19, NRSV). Sunny returned to Place of Hornets, leaving his bride of just one week—the woman who had been so right for him—back in the town of Allotted Portion.

Oh, we must note one more thing at this point. Sunny's "wife then married one of those who had been his wedding companions" (verse 20, Tanakh). That surely was rubbing salt into his wounds! But Sunny was not yet aware of what had taken place down there in Allotted Portion.

One can't remain irate indefinitely, and after some time had passed Sunny's anger subsided. It was now harvesttime for the wheat crops—sometime between mid-May and mid-June. Deciding that he'd better go back down to the town of Allotted Portion and make up with his new wife, he even brought her a baby goat as a present. Maybe back then a kid was the equivalent of a dozen roses or a box of chocolates. I don't know.

But Sunny was in for a rude awakening. His father-in-law wouldn't let him into the house! "But I want to go into the bedroom with her," Sunny protested.

The father-in-law explained, "I was sure that you had rejected her; so I gave her to your companion" (Judges 15:2, NRSV). One of the 30 men who had accompanied Sunny during the seven-day drinking party got the bride! (You can see here what happens in a patriarchal society. Women are like pieces of property that can, upon whim, be transferred from one man to another.)

But the father-in-law had a concession. "Isn't her younger sister more attractive? Take her instead" (see verse 2). Hey, why not marry the prettier girl of the two? But Sunny wanted nothing of it. Managing to trap 300 foxes, he tied a lighted torch between the tails of every two animals, and sent them running through the farmland. Now instead of the bride's home being consumed by arson, he incinerated the Philistines' crops for the year, burning "up the shocks and the standing grain, as well as the vineyards and olive groves" (verse 5, NRSV).

When the Philistines found out that Sunny had done it, he regained his honor, but they lost even more of their honor, for he had put them to shame. Their anger switched from him to the father-in-law, and they burned down his home (verse 6). So the bride's home ended up destroyed by arsonists after all, and both father and daughter perished in it!

Such blood feuds were not easily resolved in the ancient Near East. Instead they kept escalating as each aggrieved party tried to regain lost honor in a vicious circle of violence. And that's what happened in this story.

Now Sunny felt that he must avenge the honor of his father-in-law's family. So he told the Philistines living in Allotted Portion, "If this is what you do, I swear I will not stop until I have taken revenge on you" (verse 7, NRSV). Not a good scene at all, especially when Sunny, the one-man army, is involved. True to his word, he "smote them hip and thigh with a great slaughter" (verse 8). Some scholars think that the narrator is using wrestling terminology here.

Then Sunny went down to hide out in the cave of the cliff of Etam ("place of birds of prey"). There he managed to reach a nearly inaccessible cave in a cliff, where, like an eagle, he could keep an eye on all that took place below him. High ground was always advantageous in battles, and Sunny must have known that the cycle of vengeance had not yet exhausted itself.

Sure enough, danger threatened again. This time the threat came only indirectly from the Philistines. The Philistines attacked the Judahites, who when they learned the reason for the raid, decided to fetch Sunny on their own. Some 3,000 Judahites tracked him down to capture him and turn him over to the Philistines. Perhaps such a deed would put an end to the blood feud between Sunny and the Philistines.

Three thousand warriors sounds like an oversized mob to capture a lone man. It may not have been that many, though, because the Hebrew word translated "thousand" can also be translated "contingent," which some scholars estimate consisted of from 8 to 14 troops (see Gregory Mobley, *The Empty Men*, pp. 35, 36).

Talking to the Judahites, people who should have been on his side, Sunny managed to extract a vow from them that they wouldn't hurt him but merely capture him and hand him over to the Philistines. Then he let them nab him, and they tied him up with two new ropes. (Two new ropes will appear again later in the story.)

When the Judahite troops neared the town of Lehi ("jawbone"), the townspeople raced out to meet them, shouting epithets at Sunny. Once again the Spirit of YHWH flowed over him—bad news for the people from the town of Jawbone. Suddenly supernaturally strong, Sunny broke the cords that bound him. "The ropes that were on his arms became like flax that has caught fire, and his bonds melted off his hands" (verse 14, NRSV). Then he saw lying on the ground an ass's jawbone—an amazing find at the town of Jawbone! Sunny swung the jawbone (the magical gimmick that would help him prevail) as if it were an offensive weapon, and 1,000 men— or an entire contingent—lay dead in the dirt (verse 15). After this remarkable slaughter, Sunny sang a little ditty to celebrate his feat of daring:

"With the jawbone of a donkey,

heaps upon heaps,

with the jawbone of a donkey

I have slain a thousand men" (verse 16, NRSV).

The "heaps upon heaps" or "One heap! Two heaps!" uses another pun in Hebrew. The Hebrew word for "heap" and for "donkey" are identical.

After such prodigious effort, Sunny became terribly thirsty. But where could he find water? Well, his James Bondesque tool—the donkey's jawbone, which he had cast aside as no longer useful—turned into a drinking fountain. "God clave an hollow place that was in the jaw, and there came water thereout" (verse 19). And "his spirit [Sunny's, not YHWH's Spirit] returned, and he revived" (verse 19, NRSV).

(The Hebrew text is unclear whether the water came from the donkey's jawbone or from the town of Jawbone. It merely indicates that it came from jawbone/Jawbone. If the former is correct, as in the KJV, then it is very James Bondesque. But if the latter is the case, a miracle still took place, but the effect is not as outlandish as the former.)

End of Act 2 of this exciting story.

Act 3—Woman Number 3—The third act opens with the simple words "Samson went to Gaza" (Joshua 16:1, RSV). The city of Gaza ("fortress") was the largest and southernmost city belonging to the Philistines. It was about 30 miles from where Sunny had performed his other escapades, so it was new enemy territory for YHWH's not-so-secret agent. Scripture does not explain why he would travel to such a stronghold.

Apparently it didn't take him long to discover one of the prostitutes living in Fortress (verse 1). The Hebrew uses two words here to describe the person—"a harlot woman" or "a woman, a harlot." The verb and syntax of the sentence can be translated "he entered her." Whether the Hebrew contains a sexual overtone—an erotic circumlocution—we don't know. It's certainly possible . . . and maybe probable, given Sunny's predilection for sexual dalliances.

While Sunny was enjoying himself with the harlot, the locals somehow learned of his presence and decided that it was the ideal time to get even once and for all with the troublesome young man. Quietly some of the men living in Fortress hid themselves in the town's gate. How do people hide inside a gate? In addition to being constructed from heavy timbers, city gates also included anterooms on both sides of the entrance—little rooms in which people could conduct business or in which the authorities posted guards. Although small and cramped, they served nicely for the purpose for which they were constructed. Such two-story gate structures were the only way someone could enter a city, yet they had to be strong so that hostile forces could not easily breach them.

All night long the men hid in the anterooms of the gate, lying in wait for Sunny, who surely would eventually have to exit the city. As the long hours passed they kept whispering to one another—possibly to maintain their courage—"In the morning, when it is day, we shall kill him" (verse 2).

Sunny stayed in bed (presumably with the prostitute) until midnight (verse 3). Then unexpectedly he rose and headed for the city gate. He didn't know, of course, about the men lying in wait for him. When he got to the gate—in the dark of midnight—he "took hold of the doors of the city gate and the two posts, pulled them up, bar and all, put them on his shoulders, and carried them to the top of the hill that is in front of Hebron" (verse 3, NRSV).

Some picture Sunny carrying just the wooden gate on his back, which may well have been the case. But it may be that he was carrying the whole structure—wooden gate and its anterooms—on his shoulders. If that's the case, then it is truly a comical situation. Sunny was carrying not only the timber but also the little gatehouses with the men inside. Can't you just imagine those men wondering why all of a sudden they felt tossed about? It was as though they were in an earthquake, jostled from one side to the other as Sunny stomped all the way uphill to Hebron ("covenant place")—nearly 40 miles away. What a ride! How Sunny could manage to traipse so many miles—uphill—with either just a wooden gate or the entire gate complex balanced on his shoulders is anyone's guess, because the biblical author doesn't tell us here that the Spirit of YHWH had rushed over him.

End of Act 3.

Act 4—Woman Number 4—You'd think that by now Sunny would have had his fill of dalliances with the opposite sex. But he seems to have been a slow learner. We next find him in the Valley of Sorek ("bright-red choice grapes"), a locale not far from his home. But what was Sunny doing in the Valley of Bright-Red Choice Grapes? That was no place for a Nazirite.

Well, we soon find out—he'd fallen in love! The siren's name was Delilah ("flirt"). It may also be a pun on the Hebrew word for night, whereas his is a pun on the Hebrew term for sun. Philistine leaders approached her—the assumption is that she too was a Philistine—and asked her to find out for them why Sunny was so invincible. They wanted her to do exactly what the 30 Philistines had asked his bride to do—to open herself to him, which means to seduce him (Judges 16:5). They also explained to her why they wanted the information: "So that we may bind him in order to subdue him" (verse 5, NRSV).

Rather than threaten her with dire consequences if she didn't comply with their wishes (as did the 30 Philistine men at Sunny's wedding party), they offered Miss Flirt a monetary bribe: "We will each give you eleven hundred pieces of silver" (verse 5, NRSV). If the Philistine leaders (sometimes translated as "tyrants") hailed from each of the five Philistine cities, then Miss Flirt would end up with 5,500 pieces of silver—a massive amount of wealth, especially for a woman. Much earlier Abraham had paid only 400 shekels for the Cave of Machpelah and the surrounding land (Gen. 23:15, 19), and later Jeremiah paid only 17 shekels for a piece of real estate (Jer. 32:9).

The story doesn't report what Miss Flirt said to the Philistine rulers, but it does tell us what she did, from which we can infer that she agreed to the deal. "Please tell me what makes your strength so great, and how you could be bound, so that one could subdue you" (verse 6, NRSV), she asks Sunny. Not beating around the bush, Miss Flirt broached the topic in an up-front manner.

Sunny, however, wasn't very straightforward with her. In fact, he outright lied, when he replied, "If they bind me with seven fresh bowstrings [or tendons or guts] that are not dried out, then I shall become weak, and be like anyone else" (verse 7, NRSV).

Miss Flirt wasted no time in informing the Philistine leaders, who procured seven strands of unprocessed animal gut. While they hid in her room, she proceeded to tie up Sunny with the raw gut. Then in a quavering voice she announced, "Philistines, Sunny!"

Immediately—without the Spirit of YHWH coursing over him—Sunny snapped the bindings as if they were burnt flax threads (verse 9).

Sunny must have taken it all as a joke, but Miss Flirt acted as though he'd hurt her feelings. "You have mocked me and told me lies; please tell me how you could be bound" (verse 10, NRSV).

In response he spun another yarn: "If they bind me with new ropes that have not been used, then I shall become weak, and be like anyone else" (verse 11, NRSV).

The narrator doesn't give us any clue as to the passage of time, but somehow, somewhere Miss Flirt obtained brand-new ropes. She used them to tie up Sunny. (What kind of fool was he? Hadn't he been through this little routine before? Didn't he know what would happen next? Maybe he didn't care, viewing the whole thing as an amusing game.) Then she said the same words she'd uttered earlier: "Philistines, Sunny!"

Again Sunny broke his bonds as though they had been threads rather than ropes, and again Miss Flirt accused him of lying to her.

Once more Sunny told his lover a tall tale. "If you weave the seven locks of my head with the web and make it tight with the pin, then I shall become weak, and be like anyone else" (verse 13, NRSV). Here we learn that because Sunny had never had his hair cut, he wore it in seven dread-locks. (Carvings from ancient Mesopotamia portray some men with six dreadlocks. So a style now popular among African-Americans is hardly new!) He told Miss Flirt that if she wove his seven dreadlocks into a piece of cloth still in the loom, he'd be just as weak as any other man.

Once more, without any clues as to passage of time, we find Sunny asleep in Miss Flirt's house. She deftly wove his dreadlocks into the warp of a piece of cloth still on the loom. The posts of the loom had been fit-ted into deep holes in the ground to keep the loom upright and firm. Should the prostrate Sunny wake up and try to escape, he'd find himself firmly attached to the cloth, which in turn was firmly affixed to the loom, which in turn had posts securely planted in the ground. Surely she had Sunny caught this time!

"Philistines, Sunny!" Miss Flirt shouted loudly enough that it awak-ened him from his deep sleep. And when he wrenched himself from his prone position, he pulled up the entire loom and its contents. It must have been an amusing sight. Interestingly, this time the narrator doesn't tell us that Philistines were hiding in ambush in the house. Maybe Miss Flirt was wising up—faster than Sunny was—and decided not to involve them on her third attempt. Or maybe the Philistine tyrants had gotten tired of the game and decided to absent themselves this time around.

"How can you say, 'I love you,' when your heart is not with me? You have mocked me three times now and have not told me what makes your strength so great" (verse 15, NRSV).

The story is getting a bit boring, isn't it? It's all so repetitive. (But re-member that most people in the biblical world would have heard the nar-rative recited, not read it. And repetition is a strong and vital part of oral storytelling.)

But Miss Flirt kept riding Sunny to the point that he felt "tired to death" (verse 16, NRSV). She wore him down until he finally told her the truth. "A razor has never come upon my head; for I have been a nazirite to God from my mother's womb. If my head were shaved, then my strength would leave me; I would become weak, and be like anyone else" (verse 17, NRSV).

Maybe it was the tone of his voice or maybe it was a woman's intuition, but whatever it was, Miss Flirt decided that this time Sunny had told the truth. "When [Miss Flirt] realized that he had told her his whole secret, she sent and called the lords of the Philistines, saying, 'This time come up, for he has told his whole secret to me.' Then the lords of the Philistines came up to her, and brought the money in their hands" (verse 18, NRSV).

Miss Flirt must have ogled the shekels in their hands—maybe as much as 5,500 shekels of silver! So she had Sunny lay his head with its seven dreadlocks in her lap, and she lulled him to sleep. Once he was out to the world, she called in a barber "and had him shave off the seven locks of his head. [Sunny] began to weaken, and his strength left him" (verse 19, NRSV). He must have been a sound sleeper, because he didn't awaken even while the barber turned his head this way and that during the shaving process.

After the dastardly deed was done, Miss Flirt again sounded the alarm: "Philistines, Sunny!"

As those three times before, Sunny jumped up, confident that he'd have his unusual strength to deliver him from whatever danger was lurking, but . . . "he did not know that the Lord had left him" (verse 20, NRSV).

The Philistine tyrants captured Sunny and gouged out his eyes, a common procedure done on prisoners of war in the ancient Near East. (Eyes, I'm told, with just a little pressure in the outside corners will pop right out of a person's head. It's a self-defense tactic sometimes taught to women today. However, in the ancient Near East the method most often used was to burn the eyes with a hot iron or puncture them with a sharp tool.) They marched Sunny to Gaza and put him in bronze shackles. Imprisoned and sentenced to hard labor, "he ground at the mill in the prison" (verse 21, NRSV), doing the job of a donkey or an ox. (Other commentators suggest that he was using a saddle quern, the grinding tool of a woman. They had reduced the super he-man to the role of a woman.)

Again we may see here a double entendre. It's clear that Sunny had to push the mill wheel around or the saddle quern back and forth to grind the grain. But grinding was also a Hebrew euphemism for coitus, something that Sunny seemed to do quite often . . . and with different women.

We hear no more about Miss Flirt, who now disappeared—with her 5,500 shekels of silver, we presume—from Act 4.

Time went by. How much, we don't know. But Sunny's hair began growing back, and somehow the Philistines hadn't taken this possibility into consideration. But surely it was inevitable that his hair would return over time.

Then came a special day. The Philistine rulers were going to have a celebration. They would offer a colossal sacrifice to their god Dagon. It would be an occasion full of joy, full of laughter, full of happiness (verse 23). But it also would be a celebration that would go down in history as one of the most memorable ever.

And it was!

The crowd of ecstatic worshippers began chanting, "[Dagon] has given [Sunny] our enemy into our hand" (verse 23, NRSV). Somehow—the narrator doesn't give us any details—the crowd saw Sunny and went crazy, shouting, "Our god has given our enemy into our hand, the ravager of our country, who has killed many of us" (verse 24, NRSV).

Finally the revelers demanded that Sunny be brought center stage so that he could entertain them. A servant boy brought the blind prisoner out where he could give the crowd of some 3,000 people (verse 27) a good laugh.

Amid the jollity and jeering, Sunny, feigning weariness, asked the servant boy to let him lean on the pillars that supported the temple. (Perhaps he'd seen them during some of his earlier escapades in Gaza. Such pillars were a common feature of Philistine and other temples of Palestine.) He then offered a short prayer to YHWH: "Lord God, remember me and strengthen me only this once, O God, so that with this one act of revenge I may pay back the Philistines for my two eyes" (verse 28, NRSV).

Wrapping his arms around the two central pillars, Sunny pulled mightily, as he cried, "Let me die with the Philistines" (verse 30, NRSV). At first, I suspect, nothing happened, but soon he could feel (and perhaps hear) a slight shivering as the pillars and the structure they supported began to shift. A louder scraping sound followed. Probably by that time the roars of the crowd had segued into screams of terror as the balcony they were seated on started to tilt. Then the whole edifice collapsed, followed by moans from the dying—and Sunny was among the casualties.

The narrator coolly observes that "the dead which he slew at his death were more than they which he slew in his life" (verse 30).

Now at the end of his life—and at the end of the story—we learn that

Sunny had siblings—brothers. That's something we'd not heard earlier in the narrative. They and Mr. Rest Secure's household "came down" (verse 31) to Gaza, carried Sunny's crushed body back "up" to Place of Hornets, and they buried him in a tomb located somewhere between Place of Hornets and Eshtaol ("narrow pass").

"And he judged Israel twenty years" (verse 31).

End of Act 4. End of story.

In Closing

OK, what do we make of this intriguing story? I can imagine a group of Israelite men squatting around a campfire, the older men regaling the younger ones with stories from the past. In such settings it's only normal to expect the narrators to relate tales of derring-do. I can hear one of them say, "Did I ever tell you about Sunny and what he did to the Philistines?" He'd then launch into the story of Samson's weeklong marriage to the young woman from the town of Allotted Portion.

"Aw, that's nothing," another retorts. "Why, one day Sunny went down to Fortress." And he would relate the story in all both its gory and drolly comical details.

A third can hardly wait for his turn. "And don't forget the time Sunny brought the house down."

The men—especially the younger ones, aspiring Hebrew hulks—tittered and guffawed at the accounts that tingled their imaginations. Yes, in bed or out of it, Sunny was a force to reckon with.

But that still ignores the important question: Why a cycle of such earthy and titillating stories in the Bible? Surely they are included to do more than provide fodder for campfire tales about a strong man with a moral backbone weaker than a strip of toothpaste! Like James Bond, Agent 007, Sunny makes a marvelous hero for secular-minded people, but why should God's people back then—and today—read about his exploits? Surely the tales of Sunny's antics are not for converted men and women!

Nevertheless, Scripture preserves them. Obviously Sunny was not merely someone whom the ancient Israelites tolerated. No, he was one of Israel's great leaders! Yes, you may reply, but that was in Old Testament times, when men were earthy and women were lusty. But wait! His name also appears in the New Testament—engraved on the honor roll of faith in Hebrews 11. Strange. Very strange. Here was a man who seemed to have been bereft of moral force, yet God made him a hero!

We're not alone in wondering about the value of including such narratives in Sacred Writ. Biblical scholars—academics—have asked the same question. Some have suggested that they show us the dangers of love and sex—or is it sex and love? J. Cheryl Exum proposes that they teach us that God answers prayers, because at least twice in the story cycle someone offers prayers and God answers them. Others wonder if perhaps these page turners are there because they had a political message, because Sunny began to fight—and King David later ended the struggle—Philistine domination of the Hebrew people.

Here's something else for you to consider. Although most of us are no "Incredible Hulks" as Sunny must have been, we do from time to time suffer from a lack of inner moral fortitude—despite our best intentions. It's embarrassing to admit, but most of us recognize that sometimes we seem to have the spiritual rigidity of a wet strip of tissue paper. So maybe we resemble Sunny more than we think.

And perhaps that is why the Bible includes the story.

Roman Catholic priest Andrew M. Greeley (also a trained sociologist) has written novels about morally weak persons. What he gives as his reason for writing what he calls "religious" books may give us insight into why Scripture preserved the stories about Samson. Greeley says that his stories—at times lurid as they may be—"will be successful if the reader" learns that "God . . . draws straight with crooked lines."

Now that's something to think about! God, through His grace, can turn the crooked lines that we make with our lives into straight ones—just as He did with Samson's moral ineptitude. Even though Sunny was not an ethical model, God still used him as a judge—and savior—of ancient Israel.

And God still uses imperfect people—you and me, earthy though we may be. He miraculously—and graciously—"draws straight with [our] crooked lines."

CHAPTER 16

Story Time—
Who Is the Good Samaritan?

T he annual meeting of the Society of Biblical Literature had con-
vened in San Francisco. It can be quite cool in northern California
during November—especially after the sun goes down or before it is fully
up. But regardless of the weather, several thousand scholars—New
Testament scholars, Old Testament scholars, and systematic theologians—
thronged the side streets and clogged the lobbies and elevators of the hotels.
Also in attendance were a few thousand students of religion—members of
the American Academy of Religion.

Such annual meetings are like a convention of theologians of various
religions—Protestant, Jewish, Roman Catholic, Greek Orthodox,
Buddhist, Zoroastrian, Hindu. Even agnostic scholars attend. Hundreds of
scholarly papers get read and critiqued and responded to. Large ballrooms
and tiny, almost closetlike rooms overflow with participants. Some sit
around tables or on rows of disorganized chairs. Others crouch on the floor
or stand in the hallway and hover as close to the door as possible. And the
pièce de résistance of the whole thing is the book display, where scholars
can purchase theological tomes at 20, 30, 40, and 50 percent discounts.

One early, cool morning I was walking briskly several blocks to reach
a small restaurant where I could eat breakfast at a fraction of the cost back
in the hotel dining rooms. On the way I noticed a form draped in ragged
clothing and curled up into a near-fetal position in an outside entryway. A
paper bag or two lie crumpled near his head. The man's face was barely
visible, but it was clear that he hadn't shaved or washed in a long time. He

must have felt very uncomfortable after having spent the night curled up on that cold stone doorstep.

A bit fearful of this unkempt being lying barely off the sidewalk, I hurried by. Maybe he was dangerous. Perhaps he was a drug addict. Possibly he was insane. I diverted my eyes, not wanting to embarrass the man—or myself. So I hastened on my way and ate my breakfast of cheese omelet and hash browns and milk and then retraced my steps back to the hotel, where the meetings would begin at 9:00.

As I again neared the spot where the derelict was lying, I noticed ahead of me one of the liberal scholars attending these meetings (and believe me, some of these scholars are extremely liberal in their theological perspectives). In his hand he clutched a small bag from McDonald's. He stopped by the old man, gently touched him on the shoulder, and handed him the brown sack, which obviously contained a McMuffin or something like it so that the street person could have a bit of breakfast.

It was like a slap in my face. There I was—the "orthodox" minister and editor—shunning a man in need who'd been helped by someone far less conservative than I! Most likely everything I held to, this scholar probably denied. Inspired Bible—come on, who accepts that anymore? Miracles—who believes in the supernatural anymore? Jesus is divine—isn't that as superstitious as believing that a Roman emperor was god? Yet this liberal scholar provided a meal for this hungry brother on the door stoop. And I was passing by, offering not so much as a nickel or dime! Of the two of us, who was truly religious? truly spiritual? truly following in Jesus' footsteps?

In the previous chapters we explored the story of the Akedah, the binding of Isaac on Mount Moriah, and the story cycle about Samson. In this chapter we'll look at a New Testament story, the narrative commonly known as the parable of the "good Samaritan." Jesus told the anecdote, and we'll try to read it with alertness, using some of the techniques employed by what scholars call narrative criticism or narrative theology.

Pet Themes

Have you noticed that most preachers have one topic that they especially enjoy speaking about? In sermon after sermon they return to the same pet idea. For example, Martin Luther's favorite theme was justification by faith.

Jesus also had a special theme. His pet topic was the kingdom of God or the kingdom of heaven. He began story after story with the words "The kingdom of heaven is like . . ." Because of this pattern, some scholars have concluded that even when Jesus did not use that terminology to introduce a parable, the story nonetheless was about the topic dear to His heart—the kingdom of heaven. (The Jews frequently used the term *heaven* as a circumlocution for God. Most students of the Gospels believe that it was the case with Jesus. When He spoke about the kingdom of heaven, He really meant the kingdom of God.)

One of Jesus' breakthrough emphases was that the kingdom of God/heaven was present—was here—now. Sometimes He said that the kingdom of heaven was near or at hand. But if there might be any doubt whether Jesus meant close but not yet arrived, He also said that the exorcisms He performed meant that "the kingdom of God has come to you" (Luke 11:20, NRSV; cf. Matt. 12:28). Notice the tense that He used—"the kingdom *has come* to you." (Jesus also spoke of the kingdom as coming in the future. Scholars often refer to this double emphasis as "the now" and "the not yet.")

It's not surprising, therefore, that certain biblical scholars insist that *all* Jesus' parables originally dealt with the topic of the kingdom of God—including the story of the good Samaritan. At least that will be our assumption in this experiment of interpretation. In our exploration of the story about the good Samaritan, we'll operate from the presupposition that when Jesus first told the story He was trying to get across an important idea about God's kingdom.

Now let's turn to the story itself, examining the various clues in the narrative that will help unfold its meaning. We'll try to pay attention to the details, expanding their significance as we move along.

The People in the Story

In Luke 10:30-35 we encounter four travelers. So let's consider these actors first.

Jesus calls traveler number one a "certain man." Although we don't know his name or nationality, we generally assume that he was a Jew, which is a safe guess. All we know is the route he was taking. This "certain man" was hiking the Jericho Road.

Now, traveling alone was not recommended in biblical times, especially along the infamous Jericho Road, but this "certain man" was hoofing it on his own. We don't know why this "certain man" had no traveling companions. Maybe an emergency drew him to Jericho. The narrative is silent about motivation, which shouldn't come as a surprise to us. In biblical narrative one most often has to infer motive from what the characters say and do. The biblical narrator gives little insight into the psychological state of the characters. In fact, during the first century, exploring one's psyche would have been a bizarre idea. In dyadic societies a person was concerned about how others perceived him or her, not about one's own self-image. An individual's self-image depended largely on the views of others.

Traveler number two was a priest. In New Testament times Jewish society had so many priests that they had to take turns fulfilling their priestly routines at the Temple. Priests, by the way, were not on poverty row, as were most Palestinians. The Temple rites provided them with mountains of sheepskins taken from the sacrifices, and we find some indication in early sources that they did a lucrative business marketing the pelts of sheep and goats. And because the priests had to eat portions of some sacrifices, they—unlike most people of the time—had a diet rich in meat. Their high intake of flesh food caused many priests to have poor health.

Although the Temple services required an animal sacrifice, most Jews couldn't take along a sheep or goat on their treks to Jerusalem from far-flung areas of Palestine and beyond. So as a convenience to worshippers, animals specially bred to be without blemish and acceptable for holy rites were sold in the outer courts of the Temple. Historical evidence suggests that members of the priesthood benefited monetarily from the sale, on the Temple premises, of such sacrificial animals.

Ancient records indicate an enclave of priests living in Jericho. It's quite likely that this particular priest was on his way home after having taken his turn officiating at the Temple.

Traveler number three was a Levite. Like the priests, Levites had responsibilities at the Temple. And as with the priests, there was no shortage of Levites. Although they did not enjoy the same prestige as did the priests, they too were an important part of Jewish religious life. Calling them "Temple servants or staff" would probably be a fair enough description.

A Levite's livelihood depended upon what went on day after day in the Temple rituals. Indeed, a Levite's income came from tithe money, just as did the priests'. Levites also served as the musicians and gatekeepers for the Temple. They wrote and sang songs, carried Temple furniture around, cared for the Temple veils, and even killed the sacrificial animals.

Traveler number four was a Samaritan. It's possible that the Samaritan was a merchant, because he had a beast of burden, was carrying oil and wine, and had sufficient funds to pay the innkeeper in advance for a wounded traveler's care.

As is common knowledge, bad blood existed between Jews and Samaritans. In fact, it's difficult to overemphasize—or even understand—the antipathy between first-century Jews and Samaritans.

Biblical scholars do not agree as to the origins of the Samaritans. However, according to many they originated in Old Testament times during the Exile. They were half Judean and half pagan. Ultimately they ended up with their own Bible—a special version of the Pentateuch—and their own temple, with its sacred ceremonies. Later their temple was destroyed, probably by the Jewish ruler John Hyrcanus.

Samaritans liked to call themselves "*bene Yisrael*"—sons of Israel. They claimed that their name, "Samaritan," didn't come from the city of Samaria but derived from the Hebrew word *shamerim*, which means "observers"—observers of the Torah. The Jews, however, saw things quite differently. First-century Jews wanted nothing to do with Samaritans. You see, any contact with a Samaritan would render the Jew ritually unclean, which would require going through a specific ritual to become clean once again. Rabbi Eliezer said that eating with a Samaritan was the same as eating pig (Shebiith 8:10). The Mishnah charges that Samaritan women were menstruants from birth—perpetually unclean (Niddah 4:1).

We blithely speak about the *good* Samaritan, but for a first-century Judean to use the adjective "good" of a Samaritan would have been well-nigh impossible. A *good* Samaritan would be as unthinkable as a round square. It would be a nonsensical contradiction of terms—worse than an oxymoron. "Bad health" or "almost always" would have been more understandable to a first-century Jew than a "good Samaritan."

The enmity, of course, was not one-sided. Certain Hebrew religious practices were tied to the appearance of the new moon. Determination of the new moon was done visually, but sometimes the skies were cloudy, and a new observation a few days later or observations from a different locale would be used to set the time for the celebration. Judeans throughout the land would set bonfire beacons one after another when they first viewed the new moon—sort of like a relay line of Indian smoke signals. Ultimately the bonfire signals reached Jerusalem, where the Temple priests would then begin the proper services. In order to confuse the Jewish priests, the Samaritans would sometimes light bonfire signals at the wrong time.

In addition to these four travelers, Jesus' story includes some other people. It mentioned the bandits who accosted traveler number one. Bandits occupied a special category of society in first-century Palestine. They were *not* cat burglars or drug addicts in dire need of money for another fix. Most were peasants who had been so oppressed financially that they had lost everything—home and farm, hence any source of even a meager income. Such bandits typically lived on the outskirts of society and attacked those who were relatively wealthy. Frequently the peasantry admired them as heroes.

Palestine during the time of Jesus had many of these brigands, who could be quite choosy as to whom they robbed—mostly the rich. Sometimes they also had political aspirations and actually led popular uprisings. The Romans, you remember, crucified Jesus between two such bandits. And Barabbas, another bandit, had ended up killing a victim but got released instead of Jesus when the Jewish peasants—and priests—clamored for him so that Jesus would be crucified.

One other participant is all but invisible in Jesus' story—the innkeeper. We probably should not call the innkeeper an actor in the story. He really doesn't do anything other than take money from the good Samaritan. He's there simply because someone needed to run the inn. Israelite society did not hold innkeepers in high esteem.

The Backdrops in the Story

In addition to these actors in the narrative, we find two backdrops, two stage settings.

Setting number one was the road from Jerusalem to Jericho. Everyone in Jesus' audience knew about *that* road. In fact, years later Jerome referred to it as "the red and bloody way."

The distance between Jerusalem and Jericho was about 18 miles. Now, most healthy adults can walk about four miles in an hour, which would mean the trip would take a little more than four hours—if one kept hiking at a brisk pace. But in the hot Judean sun, walking that fast continuously might be asking too much. So if someone kept going at a steady three miles per hour, the traveler would be en route for about six hours. Basically it could end up being a full day's journey.

And hiking from Jerusalem to Jericho was *not* a balmy stroll. Jesus says that the unnamed man, traveler number one, was going *down* from Jerusalem to Jericho. Everyone knew what that meant. Jerusalem's altitude is nearly 2,500 feet *above* sea level. Jericho is hundreds of feet *below* sea level. So the trip involved a drop in altitude of more than 3,000 feet. The road would have a steep grade. If you had a bad knee, the journey would be pretty miserable.

Neither was it a jaunt through a cool, shady arboretum. The road wound its way through a barren, rocky, arid landscape. Think of southern Arizona with its bright—even blinding—sunlight and of temperatures in the high 90s or even in the 100s. The ecosystem of the road was, therefore, much different from that of either Jerusalem, with its olive trees, or Jericho, with its famous palm trees.

Jericho was an oasis. Watered by a copious spring, it was wonderfully fertile. It was such a delightful place that Herod built himself a luxurious winter palace there. His estate included a large sunken garden—Jericho was famous for its roses—that was 460 feet by 130 feet. He also constructed a large swimming pool—really large. Its dimensions were 138 feet by 295 feet. (An Olympic swimming pool is 82 feet wide by 164 feet long.)

One part of the Jericho Road consisted of a narrow defile threading through boulders and passing nearby caves—a cave, by the way, was where brigands loved to hang out.

Stage setting number two was that of the inn, where the good Samaritan left the injured traveler. In the ancient Near East people were not as mobile as we are today. McDonald's restaurants or Exxon gas stations or Holiday Inns did not exist every few miles. Most travelers hoped they might find distant relatives along the way. If not, Palestinian people felt obligated to care for any stranger who happened along.

Hospitality back then did not mean entertaining friends. It meant providing safe shelter and food even for total strangers. A few inns did exist, though, scattered here and there along some of the main Roman highways. About every day's journey—20 to 30 miles—there were large caravansaries, and every 10 to 15 miles a small inn might provide a modicum of shelter. But don't think of Holiday Inn or even Motel 6. Ancient inns were communal establishments to provide a little space and some food and drink for animals and people. Such caravansaries were filthy and noisy and even dangerous. Jews especially tried to avoid them, because staying at such an establishment would likely make them ritually unclean.

The Action in the Story

Now we can return to the parable itself.

A "certain man" hiked along the dangerous Jericho Road from Jerusalem. As noted previously, for whatever reason, he was doing something very dangerous—traveling an unsafe road alone instead of in the protective company of a caravan or other large group.

Suddenly he found himself surrounded by bandits who menacingly threatened him. Since such bandits were Robin Hoods who stole from the rich, it is almost certain that our unnamed Jew was fairly well-to-do. And he was an easy mark for the brigands, being alone on his journey.

So the highwaymen beat him up. Indeed, they took everything he had—even his clothing (as we noted earlier, clothing was a valuable item in the ancient world. Also Jews regarded nakedness as shameful). His nakedness now made him an object of shame in the eyes of his Jewish rivals. When the robbers ran away, he lay half dead by the side of the road—in the dust, on the rocks, in the sweltering heat—naked, comatose, bloody, sweaty, covered with buzzing and biting flies. Vultures began spiraling in tighter and ever lower circles overhead. Maybe even a bold one was already perched nearby, cocking its head to get a better look at its potential banquet.

Minutes earlier this "certain man" had been merrily, bravely, and maybe even foolishly strolling along. Now and again he'd stop and take a swig of water from his goatskin canteen. Then he'd wipe his hand across his forehead and plunge on once more. But suddenly he was brutally assaulted. And now he was lying helplessly as his life evaporated in the furnace-like heat of the day.

Although he appears to have been unconscious, we now know that the sense of hearing is the last physical sense to go. So suddenly he heard—in the dim recesses of his comatose mind—the shuffling of feet. Had the brigands returned to finish the job they'd started? He couldn't even open one eye to get a look. All he could hear was the flopping sound of sandals in the hard dirt of the road—*flip-flop; flip-flop*.

What he didn't know—but what Jesus' hearers learned—was that a priest had made the scuffing noises. Mr. Cohen—for that is the Hebrew word for priest—was on his way home from the Jerusalem Temple. In a few hours he'd be back with his family in Jericho, luxuriating in the garden-like city.

But what was that reddish hunk sprawled in the russet dirt of the roadway? Oh, no! A corpse! And a human corpse, at that! Or *was* it a corpse? What a fix! Mr. Cohen shifted from the right side of the road, where the body lay, to the left side. And passed by.

But don't be too hard on him. Remember, he was a priest, and priests were supposed to remain ritually pure—always. Mr. Cohen knew his Bible. And he was doing what was biblical. Numbers 19:11 says: "He who touches the corpse of any human being shall be unclean for seven days" (Tanakh). That biblical injunction applied to all Jews.

But another passage—Leviticus 21:1-3—applied only to priests. It says that no priest "shall defile himself for any [dead] person among his kin, except for the relatives that are closest to him: his mother, his father, his son, his daughter, and his brother; also for a virgin sister . . . for her he may defile himself" (Tanakh). Notice that it does not mention his wife as an exception. In fact, God's law specifically excluded her: "But he shall not defile himself as a kinsman by marriage, and so profane himself" (verse 4, Tanakh).

So you can't really blame Mr. Cohen, then, can you, for avoiding the comatose man by the side of the Jericho Road. He could tell at a glance that it was not his mother, not his father, not his son, not his daughter, not his brother, not his virgin sister. So he had no excuse to stop and possibly defile himself—a defilement that would last seven days—if indeed the body was a corpse.

Or was there an exception? The oral tradition included one. "If any priest, even the high priest, finds a corpse by the wayside, and there be no one in the vicinity who can be called upon to inter it, he himself must perform the burial" (*Jewish Encyclopedia*, vol. 10, p. 195). It is an exclusion known in Hebrew as *met mitzwah*.

The Mishnah states: "A High Priest . . . may not contract uncleanness because of their [dead] kindred, but they may contract uncleanness because of a neglected corpse" (Nazir 7:1). And it didn't look as if there was anyone in the area who could have buried this casualty.

But the sound of Mr. Cohen's flopping sandals got fainter and fainter as he continued on his way toward Jericho.

And so the story goes on.

Next a Levite just happened to be traveling the same route. He too had to maintain ritual purity so that he could work in the Temple. Unlike the details regarding the priest, we don't know for sure if the Levite was heading for Jerusalem or for Jericho. But it doesn't really matter, though, because if he became defiled, he wouldn't be able to eat of the tithe regardless of where he might be. And contamination from a corpse was the worst kind of defilement. The ancient religious scholars called it the "father of the fathers of uncleanness."

If he got defiled by touching a corpse, he too would remain unclean for seven days. At the end of his period of uncleanness he'd have to go through certain purging rituals. On the third and seventh days he had to be sprinkled with cleansing water, a special concoction of water and ashes from the sacrifice of a red heifer—an expensive purification solution. Then on the seventh day he would have to take a bath and wash his clothing—activities that we can do on a daily basis but that could not be as easily done during the first century. When the sun went down that evening of the seventh day, he'd be restored to a state of purity.

No, it simply wasn't worth the effort and inconvenience if the victim were dead. And it was not a simple procedure back then—as is sometimes the case even today—to determine whether or not someone was alive or dead. So the Levite, after gawking at the victim, also passed by on the other side of the road.

Once again, the flopping of the Levite's sandals became fainter and fainter. And the "certain man" continued to lie there immobile, helpless.

As luck would have it, once again the sound of footfalls penetrated his stupefied brain. This time they sounded stronger—like the clip-clops of a donkey. Although the hoofbeats grew more and more distinct, the man's unconsciousness was so deep that he could not even wish for rescue. He was terribly helpless—almost mindless.

Clip-clop.

Clip-clop.

Silence!

It was traveler number four—the Samaritan.

Jesus says in Luke 10:33 that the Samaritan had compassion on the victim. The combination of the words "Samaritan" and "compassion" must have jarred the ears of Jesus' audience. In the Hebrew Bible it was almost always *God* who showed compassion. Only rarely did Scripture indicate that a human being had compassion. And if a human did show such feeling, it was something generally reserved for relatives—kinfolk. And the Jews did *not* regard Samaritans as kin—although historically and genetically they were related.

Remember these particular details when we get ready to reveal the name and identity of the good Samaritan.

Immediately the good Samaritan went to work. He poured wine and oil into the victim's wounds. The alcohol and acidity of the wine would have acted as an antiseptic of sorts. And the olive oil would have served as a soothing emollient. The good Samaritan also wrapped the man's wounds with strips of cloth. Where he found bandages is anyone's guess. Perhaps he tore up his undergarment—his underwear.

Next the good Samaritan hoisted the victim onto his animal—most likely a donkey, which back then was the equivalent of our compact cars. If the victim was still unconscious or barely conscious, the Samaritan must have struggled with his dead weight while trying to put him on the creature—not an easy task.

After reaching the caravansary, the good Samaritan tended to the victim all night long. And the next morning when he left the inn and the injured man, he paid the innkeeper two denarii in advance. He also promised that on his return he'd settle the account should the innkeeper meet with additional expense.

A denarius was generally what a wage earner would get for a day's work. Two denarii could provide enough bread for 25 lunches. They could buy 3,000 calories of food a day for about a week for a family of four or five. Polybius, a Greek historian who lived from 203 B.C. to 120 B.C., indicated that in Italy a room at an inn would cost about 1/32 of a denarius, so two denarii could pay for about two months' lodging.

The exact coverage of the payment is not what matters, of course. What does is that the Good Samaritan was generous in his care for the injured man. He was very generous—overly so, perhaps—in his dealings with this helpless invalid whom, as far as we can tell from the story, he did not know personally. Clearly the good Samaritan saved the Jewish man's life.

The half-dead victim had been unable to dress his wounds, so the good Samaritan applied medicine and bandages. Because he had been left stark naked, we can be quite sure that his rescuer clothed him. Since the man was unable to walk, the Samaritan stranger lifted him up onto the donkey and provided transportation. After being treated mercilessly by the bandits, he now found compassion. And because he could not pay for his room and board at the inn, the good Samaritan paid it all. The half-dead traveler was passive, but the good Samaritan was active. And finally because the robbery victim was powerless to save himself, the good Samaritan saved him.

Even the religious leaders were ineffective in helping the half-dead victim, so the good Samaritan had to spring into action.

The Unifying Element in the Story

Like all stories, this one has an element running through it that ties it together. The unifying element of the story is the unnamed "certain man" who was mugged on the Jericho Road. The cast of characters includes others, and they act out the story's events in front of two backdrops. But it's the one man—the victim—who unifies the story. Although the actor who becomes the victim gives the story coherence, it's a bit of a stretch to use the verb "act" of him. Jesus employed more than 100 words to formulate the story. But only seven of those words—the first seven words of the narrative—refer to the man's actions. Throughout the rest of the story he is almost a corpse—dangerous because of his potential for defilement. His potential peril marginalized him—and rendered him dangerous in the eyes of the priest and Levite.

Such marginalization made this "certain man" an outcast. And it is this detail that helps us understand that Jesus could well have told this story about the kingdom of God.

Why?

Because He constantly taught—and lived what He preached—that it was precisely the outcasts of Judean society who were candidates for God's kingdom. As Jesus once said: "It is not those who are healthy, but those who are ill, who need the ministration of a physician." And so He surrounded Himself with the marginalized—children, women, peasants, tax collectors, prostitutes, lepers, Samaritans, those from the highways and hedges.

They were the sick who needed the physician—the people whom Jesus had come to save. That's right, the kingdom of heaven originally catered to the dregs of Judean society—not to the good people, not to the religious people, not to the righteous: not the priests, not the Levites, not the scribes, not the Pharisees, not the Sadducees.

After Jesus' death Christianity began to draw converts from the upper crust of society. Even in the book of Acts we read about priests and members of Herod's household joining the early church. And the trend continued. Today the marginalized of contemporary society don't find welcome in our sanctuaries. No, it's not like the time Jesus proclaimed the kingdom of heaven to the unwelcome ones of society.

Who are some of the marginalized in our society? They would be the homeless, the alcoholics, the women of the night, the pimps. The fellow with green or purple hair. The girl with pierced ears, nose, lips, tongue, and navel. The homosexuals.

In their presence we feel uncomfortable—even judgmental. But they are the modern equivalent of the people for whom Jesus opened the kingdom of heaven.

But they're hopeless, right?

Exactly.

No matter how handsome or good-looking, well dressed, rich, well educated, high on the social ladder, or suave we may be, when it comes to entering the kingdom of God, *we are as spiritually repugnant and unacceptable as any marginalized soul throughout history.*

Yes, we're spiritually and hopelessly ostracized.

When we read or hear a story like this, we get caught up in the narrative and can identify with any of the major characters. Perhaps we may identify with the priest, the Levite, or even with the good Samaritan. But right now we must see ourselves as the hapless victim, who had once been a vigorous and perhaps even prosperous man, and who had no second thoughts about striking out alone on the Jericho Road. Like him, you and I are the hapless victims of evil. The evil one has robbed us, beaten us, and left us naked and half dead by the side of the road.

There's nothing we can do to help ourselves. Powerless, we're barely conscious of our desperate straits. Immobile in sin, we cannot enter the kingdom of heaven unless we have help. And so the good Samaritan steps in—even when we expect help the least, despite our desperate need.

Who Is the Good Samaritan?

Before we attempt to figure out whom the good Samaritan stood for, we should make it clear that the initial point of this parable is the identification of "neighbor." Jesus told the parable in response to the question "Who is my neighbor?" (Luke 10:29, NRSV). And having finished telling the story, Jesus asked the inquirer, "Which of these three, do you think, was a neighbor to the man who fell into the hands of the robbers?" (verse 36, NRSV). And the inquirer, who may well have been a Pharisee, answered, "The one who showed him mercy" (verse 37, NRSV).

So the main point of Jesus' parable is that we should love God and love our neighbor, and our neighbor is anyone who needs help. Jesus identified "neighbor" not as someone living next door, not as a friend, not as someone with the same religious background, and not as someone sharing the same ethnicity. Anyone needing help should be regarded as the "neighbor" whom we are to love.

Having said that, though, we can look at another aspect of the story—one that several of the Church Fathers picked up on. When we read this story, we can also ask about the identity of the good Samaritan. And this aspect need not conflict with the main point that Jesus had in mind. So now let's try to figure out the identity of the good Samaritan in this parable of the kingdom—if you have not already surmised it.

Because Samaritans were of mixed ancestry, the Jews despised them. But this particular Samaritan was good. He showed compassion—an attribute generally reserved for God in the Hebrew Bible. And he did all the saving—the victim was unable to help himself.

Remember what it says in John 8:48? The Gospel record reports what some of the Judeans called Jesus: "'How right we are,' retorted the Jews, 'in calling you a Samaritan, and mad at that!'" (Phillips). Those Judeans were talking to *Jesus*. And although they made two accusations—allegedly Jesus was a Samaritan and had a devil (or was mentally ill)—He denied only the latter charge. Jesus was not, of course, a Samaritan, but He *was* of mixed heritage. He had a human lineage as well as a divine heritage.

And Jesus was the recipient of the adjective "good"—being the good Shepherd, for instance. Furthermore, the Gospels tell us again and again that He had *compassion* on the people—the same word used of the good Samaritan. Remember that in the Old Testament it's usually God who is the one who has compassion. And in the New Testament it's Jesus who most often shows compassion.

Furthermore, He covers our spiritual nakedness with the robe of His righteousness. Although we're helpless to save ourselves, Jesus can. We cannot enter the kingdom of heaven unless He transports us there.

So if indeed the parable of the good Samaritan is about the kingdom of God—and about who gets there and how—then we're safe in recognizing the amazing fact that Jesus Himself is the really truly good Samaritan, despised though He may be.

As victims, you and I have been ostracized—lost. But we have experienced His healing touch and His generosity. Jesus has taken us from a marginalized condition in sin and carried us into the kingdom of God.

A Few Words in Closing

You'll never be able to remember all that you read in these pages, but perhaps from time to time you'll recall something said here so that your study of God's Word will become more meaningful as you (1) look at the words themselves, (2) look at the grammar, (3) look at the literary context, and (4) look at the cultural context of the ancient Near East. Ask yourself what kind of language the authors of Scripture were using. (And I'm not referring to Hebrew or Aramaic or Greek, but to informative, cognitive, affective, performative, and phatic speech.)

Now in closing, I wish you God's richest blessings as you delve into His Word . . . again. My prayer is that the Bible will be even more meaningful to you as you read it.

Can we trust in the ancient writings of the Bible to express the will of God for us?

Yes, when trusted as God's Word, the Bible has the power to energize and motivate us to live the kind of lives that will glorify God. As you read the pages of *God's Book of Wisdom,* you'll be convinced that the Bible is dependable, relevant, and life-changing. 978-0-8280-2017-6. Paperback.

Discover the Bible's relevance for your life today.

Thy word is a lamp unto my feet and a light unto my path.

—Psalms 119:105

Visit your local Adventist Book Center®
- Call 1-800-765-6955
- Order online at AdventistBookCenter.com

Price and availability subject to change. Canadian price higher.

R
Review and Herald®
Publishing Association

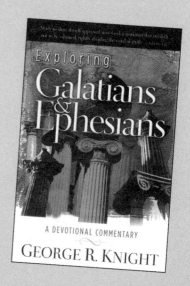

WHY DO WE NEED GOD WHEN WE SEEM TO HAVE ALL WE NEED?

Seven Reasons Why Life Is Better With God

Nathan Brown

Christianity is often styled as an answer to our problems, particularly for those who have no options left. But what about those who seem to have everything going for them? who are well off, well fed, well educated, faced with many different opportunities, and apparently doing OK?

The truth is that we don't have to hit rock bottom to need God. This book ponders seven reasons life is better with God—when things are bad, God can make them better; when things are good, God makes them better still. 978-0-8127-0436-5. Paperback, 160 pages.